D1428575

WITHDRAWN FROM
THE LIBRARY

UNIVERSITY OF
WINCHESTER

KA 0020701 2

Investigating Art

The instruction is the way and the method. The vision is the work of one who has wished to see.

Japanese proverb

Investigating Art

a practical guide
for young people

Moy Keightley

BELL & HYMAN
LONDON

Published in paperback in 1984 by
Bell & Hyman Limited
Denmark House
37-39 Queen Elizabeth Street
London SE1 2QB

First published in 1976 by Paul Elek Limited

Copyright © 1976 by Moy Keightley

All rights reserved. No part of this publication
may be reproduced, stored in a retrieval system or
transmitted, in any form or by any means, electronic,
mechanical, photocopying, recording or otherwise, without
the prior permission of Bell & Hyman Limited.

ISBN 0 7135 2446 4

Printed and bound in Great Britain
at The Pitman Press, Bath

Age of The Artists

*The numbers which appear in brackets after the description of an
example of work refer to the age of the artist.*

KING ALFRED'S COLLEGE
WINCHESTER

375.75
KEI   25188

Acknowledgements

I should like to acknowledge all the young artists who have enriched this book with their creative work. Not only have they provided individual interpretations of the projects but they have started
their own lines of enquiry, unearthing fresh clues and contributing
new ideas. I owe them my gratitude and appreciation.

Most of the work shown in the illustrations has been done by young
people independently at home. Other work, done in the studio at
school, is included with the kind permission of The North London
Collegiate School; Parliament Hill School, London; West Borough
School, Maidstone; Nonesuch High School, Cheam; The Hospital
School, Great Yarmouth; Bramcote Hills County Secondary School,
Beeston; St. Bride's School, Helensburgh.

I should like to thank Nicolette Gray and Nicholas Biddulph for
lending their photographs from the Central Lettering Record to be
reproduced on page 116; James Mosley for his photograph of a
milestone on the same page; and Geoffrey Ireland for taking the
photographs on page 141. The photograph on page 16 has been
reproduced by kind permission of the Ravens Wood School for
Boys, Bromley, Kent. The publishers are grateful to the following for
allowing the reproduction of works: National Gallery, London (page
53, 145, 148, 149, 152 and opp. p.72); Royal Library, Windsor Castle,
reproduced by Gracious Permission of H.M. The Queen (page 19);
Tate Gallery (page 20, 60, 61, 67, 143, 145, 146, 147); British
Museum (page 47); Victoria and Albert Museum (page 18, 148);
Escher Foundation, Haags Gemeentemuseum, The Hague (page 21);
Margaret Gardiner (page 23); SPADEM © 1975 (page 151).

Finally, I should like to thank my friends for their help and
encouragement; particularly Tim Shelley for reading the typescript,
Dorothy Walker for her good advice and her work in compiling the
index, Betty Lewis for her patient collaboration in typing and proof-
reading the manuscript and my editor, Janet Haffner, whose perception and understanding allowed this book to emerge.

M. K.

Jacket front Carnival. Gouache. (15)
Endpapers Inside a clock. Collage. (15)

Contents

About this book

This is a book for you to enjoy. The pictures are more important than the words, and the creative work that you do yourself is still more important.

You may think that you are not really 'any good' at art. Perhaps older people have given you the idea that you need to be born with a special kind of gift and without this you might just as well give up. This is all very misleading. One of my reasons for writing this book is to help you to see that this question of talent is not the question that really matters. If you really want to, you can grow in your understanding of art just as you can grow in your experience of any subject. You may not end up with a career as a world-famous artist just as you may not become a best-selling author because you can write stories. None of this matters. Far more important is that you should be yourself, a creative individual doing something that you enjoy.

This is what art is about. When drawing, painting, whatever you are doing, your own feelings and ideas are more important than technical cleverness. You are unique. What you do and make will never be the same as what anyone else does. So it is necessary to know how to grow and develop creatively. The nourishment that you need is all around you: it is up to you to learn how to find it.

First of all you must allow your eyes to pause and look intently. Normally our eyes do nothing of the kind, they flit superficially from object to object and are only half aware of them. The artist is a special kind of *investigator* who trains his eyes to search and discover visual 'clues'. Like a good sleuth he is interested in observing everything and selecting what is important. If you want to learn about art then this is what you must aim to do.

Once you have begun hunting in a particular direction you will find that one clue leads to another. You will begin to feel *involved* in what you are doing. This is one of the most vital ingredients in your work. Whatever you are doing, playing football, running a race, acting in a play, your involvement is what really makes things happen. Becoming absorbed in any of these activities will give you immense satisfaction. Be persistent. Don't give up when things go wrong. Of course you will meet difficulties and problems that have to be solved but this is to be expected; it applies to whatever you are studying. In fact it is just this solving of problems which can help us to be most inventive. A really creative artist is never quite satisfied with his achievement: each conclusion that he reaches is the beginning of a new exploration.

In this book you will find all kinds of starting points which will lead you towards your own visual experience. My aim has been to develop your perception and to help you to *think visually*. In this way your creative ideas will grow: you will have the key to appreciating the visual world with a new intensity and you will find yourself making your own discoveries about the language of art.

Preface for parents

My aim in writing this book is to help young people to think visually and to be aware of visual ideas. Their education at school normally directs their minds to think in other ways. For instance, in speaking, listening, writing, and reading each child lives continually in a world of words, and this naturally becomes his main mode of thought. Such an emphasis in his education is likely to restrict the growth of his visual awareness. Of course, he has his natural ability to see, but normally this ability is trained to identify things, to turn experience into words. You know how satisfying it is when a young child points to an object and hesitantly tries to say its name : these are his first steps in literacy. What I am concerned about is visual literacy. In other words, being able to think in terms of a visual language.

I have described this language in some detail in the first part of this book and suggested ways in which young people can find out more about it through their own practical work. And it should soon become clear that I do not think it very important to produce pictures which are photographically realistic. The camera does this well enough and it can be used in all kinds of inventive ways. It is about discovering the language of art and understanding how to organize it in a personal way.

I feel strongly that everyone has the capacity to be creative. Creativity is not limited to a few people with a special talent any more than is learning in other subjects. There is no need to worry about whether your child has the ability to be a professional artist or not. A few young people do leave school and eventually become famous as writers, artists or scientists, but this is incidental. After all, the purpose of education is to help the individual to develop his awareness and knowledge in a variety of ways, not just to train for a vocation.

A structured art education
In drawing and painting small children have a marvellous capacity for working without instruction from what

appears to be an endless supply of visual ideas. It is tempting to think that this spontaneous approach can be perpetuated and that older children only need to be left alone to produce art through a vague kind of 'self-expression'. This can certainly not be relied on. Young people find that all kinds of problems arise in art, and they need answers to them as much as to those that occur in other subjects. Imagination and intuition continue to play a part in all creative work but this needs to be nourished by a sense of understanding and purpose. Young people need to be taught the kind of criteria that they must use when faced with conscious choices and decisions, and I believe that art education should be structured with this in mind.

Perhaps your own art education gave you a great deal of satisfaction and helped you to think visually. Alternatively you may remember it as a series of fruitless struggles to represent objects and people so that they satisfied a vague desire for 'realism'. This kind of emphasis can be very daunting, especially as the question of realism is so complex that it can mean a variety of things. Certainly a lot of people are put off art altogether because of their inability to produce three-dimensional illusions on paper. If you were daunted it would have been more helpful if you had been encouraged to forget about illusionism and to concentrate on training your eyes to see and observe *selectively*. You will find this explained in more detail throughout the book and suffice it to say here that *discovering, analysing, assessing, manipulating,* and *translating,* are all involved. These processes help young people not only in their work at school, and in the appreciation of art generally, but in countless other ways. As you know, visual decisions will be a continuing part of their everyday adult lives. In decorating and furnishing a home, and even in cookery, we all become artists, having to solve problems about colour, shape, texture and pattern. The clothes we wear can involve us in similar choices as do all the other man-made objects of daily life.

At the same time it needs to be understood that art is not just a relaxing occupation requiring the minimum of effort. Any subject could be practised on this level but we would be disappointed with the results. Concepts have to be learned and applied in visual education just as they have to in mathematics. Those in visual education train our minds to think visually, and give us the power to express visual ideas through our grasp of visual language. Just as in a written language young people's understanding is developed through writing and reading, so in art it is developed through practical work.

Intelligent young people have the capacity to develop their perception in all kinds of ways. Unfortunately only a brief time is available for art lessons at school, perhaps no more than an hour or so a week. Preparation for other subjects eats up their spare time at home, and their visual education is likely to remain neglected. In the following sections I have made suggestions for some ways in which you can help to remedy this.

How you can help
Perhaps the most important thing when looking at the art of children is to try to understand what they are attempting to do. Naturally this will vary with different age groups. Although this book is chiefly concerned with the work of adolescents, I will begin by describing the approaches of younger children. Children up to the age of about six years, and in some cases later, are concerned with a subjective use of visual *symbols* to record things that are important to them. This means that the images that they make are not describing a house or man in the objective way in which we see them. As you know, this is a method of communication which we can easily accept when we look at maps. Special signs represent churches and bridges and other things that it would be impossible to show realistically.

You may find it quite easy to enjoy this work of very young children, but more difficult when looking at the art of the seven- to ten-year-olds. At this stage, although he is beginning to look a little more objectively, a child is still creating mainly from his own subjective experience. Remember when he shows you his drawing that you are looking at his personal ideas and that at any age he may feel a little on the defensive at showing them to you. When he shows you a picture of a sheep standing in a field resist any temptation you may have to say, 'Here, let me show you how to draw a better sheep'. This is *his* sheep standing in *his* field, not the same as the one you have in your own mind. Though sometimes he may tell you that he doesn't like what he has done, this will probably be in the hope that you will reassure him. Be appreciative and encouraging.

By about the age of eleven children begin to combine their subjective approach with a more objective awareness of their surroundings. It is still no help if you compare their drawings and paintings with your own preconceived idea of what they *should* look like. A frequent question from an adult to a child is 'What is that supposed to be?' A reaction of tolerant amusement is disturbing for children of any age. The child and the young adolescent quickly sense that you feel that his drawing is inadequate —not realistic enough. Some, through lack of confidence and embarrassment, may stop drawing altogether, while other more precocious children feel that a more photographic image would deserve your praise. They may begin to copy photographs or other artists' work in an attempt to produce some superficially sophisticated pictures. Some children retreat into a defensive position and claim that they are 'no good at art'. What they really mean is that they have failed to rise to adult expectations and standards. This negative comment needs positive help.

If he asks your advice on how to draw something from memory, encourage him to go and *look* at whatever it is and make some notes about it. The 'sheep' of the younger child now becomes the subject of visual research. In hunting for information, his eyes learn to look with a selective attitude which helps him to see more purposefully. You have the opportunity to point out *visual* qualities like the *shape* and *structure* of the head and the *texture* of the fleece. In these ways you can help him to develop his sensitivity to the language of art. His creative work is not necessarily an end in itself but a means of gradually assimilating experience.

If you have not done any drawing for some time, you will find it rather difficult to see in this way. Try to appreciate the visual values that I have mentioned; especially the way in which the individual uses *colour, shape* and *line*. If you want to discuss your child's work, do it from this *visual* point of view.

You can see what I mean if you pick up a pen and a piece of paper and begin drawing something close to you.

Let us suppose that this is a cup and saucer. As soon as marks appear on the paper, you are seeing a *translation* of these objects into a drawing. The cup and saucer become a structure of *lines* enclosing *shapes*. The terms of communication are the particular quality of the *lines,* the balance of the *shapes,* including their relationship to the edge of the paper, and perhaps the use of lines to make light and dark *tones* and *textures*.

When young children see things, they are naturally selective. They have an instinct for rejecting irrelevant details in favour of more important qualities that interest them. Unfortunately this natural selectiveness seems to become blunted as they grow older and the adolescent needs to struggle to achieve it again. You may see some mature drawings and paintings which remind you of the freshness of a childish vision. These have not been accomplished with childish ease: far from it. To achieve this kind of simplicity is extremely difficult.

Certainly the adolescent needs help in learning how to restructure his growing vision. He is developing a more objective awareness and curiosity about the world around him. This curiosity needs to be stimulated and a sensitivity to visual qualities encouraged. Just as vocabulary has to grow in a spoken language, so it needs to grow in a visual one. The key to this vocabulary is drawing: without it creative ideas dry up. I hope that this book will help to answer the eternal question, 'What shall I draw?' The problem of how to begin can be dealt with by providing sensibly structured starting points. You may wonder if such structuring is restrictive; in fact the opposite is true— it is a means of setting our minds free to be inventive. Young people enjoy purposeful problems and through solving them they begin to store up their own visual ideas.

A place to work
A very practical way in which you can encourage your child's creative development is by providing an interesting range of materials and somewhere to work.

The ideal workplace would be a spare room that could be set aside for this purpose, but space is usually too limited to allow this. The child's own room is the next best thing but it may need a little adapting. A washable floor of vinyl or lino would be practical, and a simple wooden or formica-topped table essential. Pin-up board should cover as much wall as possible (see page 11), and

some shelving and a store cupboard would be an asset.

An outside shed or a space in the garage may be another possibility, especially in summer. If there is no alternative, a corner of the kitchen or living room could be used. Paper should be spread on the table and a polythene sheet put down to protect the floor. It is better, of course, to choose somewhere which the child can make into a retreat; where he can pick up his materials and continue working without the daunting thought of having to get everything out when he wants to begin again.

Although any working area will get messy and untidy, a child should be taught to keep a reasonable sense of order. Certainly brushes have to be washed and dried, and tops screwed back on to tubes and bottles to prevent paint and ink drying up. None of this is easy to achieve. Most children are careless with their things but unless you persist in encouraging a sensitive attitude to equipment, your children will not learn how to make the most of it or to be responsible in a larger group.

Joining in
Older children are happy to work on their own, but younger ones can be encouraged if you occasionally try out ideas with them. Although this book is primarily concerned with helping adolescents, there is no reason why you should not enjoy experimenting and making things yourself. The projects suggested in *Working with friends* (page 110) could be tried by the whole family working together.

Traditional festivals provide opportunities to enrich an occasion with decorative delights and everyone can contribute something. Some of the family will enjoy making Christmas and birthday cards. I have been delighted to receive cards, divided into sections, in each of which was a drawing, pattern or collage made by different members of the family. Children often feel that their own efforts are not 'good enough' to send to friends or relations and instead they spend pocket money on expensive mass-produced cards. They can give far more pleasure by sending something, however simple, that they have made themselves.

Collecting together
As you know, almost any kind of collecting gives children pleasure. A country or seaside walk inevitably involves

seeing enticing bits and pieces that could be carried home. It is wise to go prepared with a few containers. An airtight plastic sandwich box is good for plants, plastic bags are a help in carrying damp pebbles or shells as is a strong bag or rucksack for carrying other things, like driftwood.

As well as collecting natural forms, most children enjoy cutting out pictures from magazines and pinning them on their walls or pasting them into their scrapbooks. They usually have their own ideas about what they want to collect, but you could help by suggesting a particular theme, like looking for objects within one colour range or selecting patterns and textures. This kind of collecting helps them to be visually alert and selective, and it is a good thing to encourage.

Looking at art

Another way of encouraging visual alertness is by visiting galleries and museums. Schools sometimes manage to find time to take children out on expeditions but these visits are rare, especially during examination years. If you think about it, a great deal of time is spent in introducing children to great literature but hardly any time is spent on showing them works of art. It would be a great help if you could visit exhibitions as a family group. Of course, it is not enough just to 'look' at art and leave it at that. In fact walking round a gallery or a museum can be rather an unseeing and aimless occupation, especially for children. They can be helped to look more purposefully. A few simple questions turn the passive looking into a more positive attitude of hunting for answers and this makes the visit much more enjoyable (see pages 144–55). Later, as your children grow older, encourage them to go off on a day's visit with their own friends.

Another way in which you might like to help is by providing good art books for them to browse through. Some superb and reasonably inexpensive ones have been published in the last ten years or so. If you look in your local library and bookshops you may feel inspired to build up a small art library. I would advise you to choose some biographical studies with plenty of illustrations and some that show close-up details of the work. Try to cover a wide period of time, right up to the present day. Young people need the opportunity to see contemporary art in its historical context, although much that is being done now may express ideas that we have yet to understand.

This is one of the functions of art. It is better to keep our mind open to new ideas and encourage our children to do the same rather than let our preconceived ideas be an obstacle to understanding and enjoyment.

Arranging displays

Postcard reproductions are a useful reminder of a visit to an exhibition. They are best appreciated if there is a place to display them. A pin-up board is easy to make and can be used for showing all kinds of collections. If possible, make a space in the kitchen or hall where everyone can be involved. Use a soft insulation panel, a sheet of cork, or any piece of soft board which can be nailed or screwed to the wall and painted with white emulsion or covered with felt; 6 x 4ft is a size which gives a reasonable space for a good display but it could be smaller. Dressmaking pins are less obtrusive than drawing pins.

If you have room for a table under the pin-up board, this can be used for showing three-dimensional objects. Cover it with a simple material like natural hessian, and you will see how attractive a collection of stones and other objects can look. You may want to try some direct lighting. A wall spotlight or strip light above the board can be effective.

All members of the family can help with pinning up and arranging displays and not only will it be a pleasure to look at; it will help children to develop confidence in their own work which can be pinned up too. We all enjoy the reassurance of appreciation and approval.

The importance of creativity

When you think about it, creativity is the most satisfying thing in life. Whatever one is creating, there is the pleasure of conceiving an individual piece of work and watching it grow. You also know the special satisfaction of doing something well, rather than thoughtlessly and carelessly. The Balinese have a saying, 'We have no art. We do everything as well as we can.'

This book is concerned with helping all growing people to extend their own ideas and to find enjoyment in visual things. Everyone has the ability to create: it is not for a privileged few, or limited to any age group. You can find your own creative preoccupation and help your children to do the same. If you pursue it with a sense of purpose, you will gain an endless source of satisfaction.

Equipment and materials

Perhaps you already know how enjoyable it is to browse around a shop that specializes in art equipment. The range of paint, paper and tools can be so enormous that it is difficult to know what to choose. I am going to give you a list of basic tools that will be useful to have, and some notes on different kinds of paper and paint. There is no need to get everything at once. Start with a few things and add others as you go along.

You will enjoy using some materials because they are familiar to you, but be prepared to try new ones as well. Each project described in this book includes details of the materials to be used. It is up to you to try out your own variations on these, by choosing different kinds of paper in different sizes, and, if you like, varying the other materials to suit your ideas.

Whichever materials you use, the important thing is to enjoy the *feeling* of their particular qualities. Spreading chocolate icing on a cake has a lovely feeling about it. In a similar way you can relish the feeling of paint, or crayon, or felt pen, or whatever you are using. Each material has its own character. You will discover what it is if you allow yourself to appreciate the special qualities of the materials as you use them. And you will find that it is no use trying to force one material to behave like another. Thick opaque paint applied with a palette knife cannot be made to express the same feeling as thin, transparent watercolour drifted across a piece of pure white paper. Far the best way of understanding about these methods and materials is through your own direct experience.

The ideal ingredient to add to this is *time.* If you have a place where you can work and settle down for a whole morning, you will really see results. Snatches of broken-up time are not nearly so rewarding, although it is better to use an odd half hour rather than to do nothing at all.

If you are interested in art and want to learn more about it, then try to set aside a time when you can experiment with some of the work suggested in the following pages.

In this way you will begin to understand more about the language of art, and one idea will lead you to another.

A basic tool-kit (see following pages for detailed comment)

1 *a variety of drawing tools:* pencils, HB, 2B, 4B; coloured felt-tip pens; ball-point pens; a cheap fountain pen with black ink; coloured crayons; charcoal
2 *painting equipment:* some form of paint; a thin and a medium-size soft-haired brush; a medium- and a large-size bristle brush; palette knife
3 *adhesives*
4 *scissors* and possibly a 'handyman's' *knife* with replaceable blades (i.e. 'Stanley' knife)
5 *a portfolio*
6 *a sketchbook*
7 *a drawing board.* I recommend a strong, wooden one about 24 x 16in or larger. A cheaper alternative would be a piece of thick hardboard. Use 'bulldog' clips rather than drawing pins (thumb tacks) which damage the surface.
8 materials for print-making (see page 132)
9 materials for three-dimensional work (see pages 66 and 138)

It is a good idea to have a bag for carrying equipment if you intend to go out and draw. Certainly camera enthusiasts and fishermen carry their kit-bags with them. You could use a similar kind of shoulder bag or a canvas hold-all. It needs to be large enough to hold your sketchbook and drawing materials, and any food that you want to take with you. I find that two 'bulldog' clips are invaluable for holding down pages of a notebook on a breezy day; and a newspaper or a piece of plastic might come in handy for sitting on damp ground, boring though it sounds.

Here are some detailed notes on the kinds of paper and paint that you will find to choose from.

Paper
You can draw and paint on all kinds of paper. The two

most referred to in this book are *sugar paper* and *cartridge paper* but there are others that you can try for yourself.

Paper sizes:		*millimetres*	*inches* (approx)
	A1	594 x 841	$23\frac{3}{8}$ x $33\frac{1}{8}$
	A2	420 x 594	$16\frac{1}{2}$ x $23\frac{3}{8}$
	A3	297 x 420	$11\frac{3}{4}$ x $16\frac{1}{2}$
	A4	210 x 297	$8\frac{1}{4}$ x $11\frac{3}{4}$

Sugar paper/construction paper
One of the cheapest papers available. Usually grey in colour but sometimes made in white, dark blue and other subdued colours. Use for opaque paints, i.e. powder paint, gouache and acrylic, not transparent watercolour. Draw on it with chalks, charcoal or crayons. Also makes a good base for collage.

Cartridge paper/drawing paper
Less absorbent and more closely woven paper. Usually white or cream in colour. Sold in a range of thicknesses, the thicker the paper the greater the cost. Use with any materials. Makes a good surface for watercolour (i.e. transparent paint) and for drawing with pencils, pens and crayons.

You may have noticed the tendency of cartridge paper to buckle up when you apply water to it: here is a simple method of stretching the paper to avoid this. All you need is a board, a sponge and a roll of brown gummed strip, (packing tape) 1 in wide.

1 Soak the paper in clean water by saturating both sides with a sponge.
2 Spread the wet paper on to a clean drawing board and soak up excess water with a sponge or blotting paper.
3 Cut the gummed strip into four lengths to fit the paper and wet the gum thoroughly.
4 Fix all four edges of the paper firmly to the board with the gummed strips (packing tape).

As the paper dries it will stretch flat. When it is completely dry you can paint on it without the surface buckling. Cut the paper free from the gummed strips when you have finished.

Detail paper
A thin white paper sometimes called Bank or Typewriting paper. Cheap and useful for fine pen-drawings, for making rubbings and as a tracing paper. Economical to buy packs of 500 sheets sold for typing.

Newsprint
Another really cheap paper but difficult to obtain unless ordered through an art supplier in packets of 1 ream (500 sheets). Use for drawing with charcoal, crayons and paint and all kinds of printing.

Old newspapers
These are made from newsprint. You can use them as a base for really thick painting.

Brown wrapping paper
Sold in large sheets which are useful for making murals. Use for thick powder paint and as a base for collage.

Coloured paper
Made in all kinds of surface textures: glossy, matt, patterned, embossed, etc. Collect for collages.

Coloured tissue paper
Made in vivid colours. Use for printing from lino (linoleum) blocks and making collages.

Cardboard
Cardboard discarded from packaging can be saved and used for making constructions or as a surface for painting.

Strawboard
This is the cheapest cardboard to buy. Sandy yellow in colour, with a soft, absorbent surface. Sold in a range of thicknesses.

White card/poster board
Smooth, refined surface. Sold in a range of thicknesses (i.e. 2 sheet card = thin, 4 sheet = thicker). Use for drawing with all kinds of materials and for making constructions.

Paint
The paints most referred to in this book are *powder paint* and *gouache* but there are other kinds of paint which you can try for yourself, and which you will see on sale in an art shop.

Powder paint

Sometimes called *tempera colour.* This is the cheapest paint to buy. It is sold in tins of various sizes. The largest sizes are the most economical. The powder mixes easily with water to a variety of consistencies. For details of colours to choose, see page 38. Keep the colours in separate paper baking-cases in a bun tray and use another bun tray for mixing. This paint is also sold in small, solid discs. These should be well moistened before use as it takes longer to build up the same richness of paint.

Gouache

Sometimes called *poster paint* or *designer's colour.* Sold ready mixed in tubes and jars. Paint squeezed from tubes and not used dries hard and has to be thrown away. Jars are therefore a better idea but the paint will dry hard unless lids are screwed on after use: it also helps to add a little water as the jar empties. The quality of colour is more intense than in powder paint. It dries to a smooth, matt finish and is particularly suitable for painting on a small scale.

Watercolour

Unlike powder paint and gouache, this paint dries with a transparent quality leaving the paper showing through the colour. Sold in boxes of tiny rectangular blocks or small tubes. Only buy boxes sold by a reputable art supplier. Those sold in toyshops, with rows of colours, are too hard and frustrating to use.

Acrylic paint

This has a quick-drying plastic base, similar to household emulsion paint. Sold under a variety of trade names. Paint mixes with water and dries smooth and matt like gouache. A gloss finish can be achieved with the addition of an acrylic medium. Can be painted on to any surfaces (canvas, wood, hardboard as well as paper) and when dry it is no longer soluble in water. Wash brushes immediately after use to prevent paint hardening in the bristles.

Oil paint

For the work in this book I have not encouraged the use of oil colour because there is rather more preparation and cleaning up to be done than with other materials. However, if you want to, you can use it whenever you like as an alternative to powder paint. Some people think that there is a special mystique about oil paint and believe that you must be taught *how* to use it. In fact you can use it like any other paint. All paints are made of pigments, but whereas powder paint, watercolour and gouache are bound with gum and are therefore water soluble, oil paint is bound with oil and therefore is soluble only in turpentine. Unlike powder paint and gouache the colour does not lighten when it dries but it does dry far less quickly.

You need a flat surface to squeeze the colours on to and this can be a palette, a piece of formica, a slab of glass or just a strip of hardboard. Mix the colours with a palette knife and, if you like, use the knife for painting, or work with bristle brushes. It does help to have several brushes so that you can use colours without having to wash your brush each time. The paint can also be used more thinly by diluting it with turpentine. This tends to reduce the glossiness of the paint: if you want to keep this quality, add an equal quantity of linseed oil to the turpentine.

Choose 'student's' quality rather than 'artist's' because oil is more expensive than water-based paints; and buy large tubes or tins. Use on strong paper, cardboard, hardboard, wood, or canvas. To prevent the oil from soaking in, the surface must be made non-absorbent by sealing with a coat of size (thin glue) or polycell. When this is thoroughly dry, white undercoat paint can be applied if you want to paint on a white surface. Instead of using size, an alternative method is to apply one or two coats of white acrylic paint. Leave at least two hours between coats and allow the final coat to harden for twenty-four hours before painting on it.

You will have more cleaning up after a session of using oil paint but the delicious smell of the oil and the turpentine makes up for this. Rinse the paint from your brushes with turpentine and then lather them up with soap and cold water (warm water tends to soften the glue holding the bristles in place) until all the colour disappears. Finally rinse them in clear water, dry and smooth back into shape. Scrape up any paint left on your palette and wipe clean with a rag.

Coloured inks

Instead of using paint you may like to experiment with coloured inks. Used on white paper these produce fine, rich, glowing colours. They can be intermixed or, being waterproof, applied in thin layers of one wash of colour over another.

Coloured crayons, pencils and pastels

These materials provide colour in a convenient form and are useful for carrying with you if you want to work outside. They can be used in all kinds of ways to make flat or textured surfaces or superimposed on each other to produce new colours.

All the materials that I have described, except oil-bound pigment, can not only be used by themselves but also in combination with each other.

Brushes

Although you will find that brushes are expensive it is always better to buy a good quality brush which will be pleasant to use and will last a long time, rather than a cheap, inferior one.

Bristle or hog-hair

These are made either round or flat in section, and in a variety of thicknesses. The flat section brushes, about $\frac{1}{2}$in wide, are the most useful ones. You will sometimes need brushes smaller and larger than this, so try to collect several different ones. Use with any paint.

Soft-haired brushes

These are made of squirrel, camel, ox and sable hair. The sable brushes are the most flexible and the easiest to control but they are particularly expensive. A reasonable substitute is a brush made of a blend of ox and sable hair. Useful sizes are thin size No. 2 and medium size No. 5 or 6. Use for any paint, especially gouache and watercolour. All brushes should be washed thoroughly in cold water after use, dried and smoothed back into shape.

Palette knives

Most art suppliers stock a wide range of shapes: the simplest 'knife' shape, about 3in long, is the cheapest and quite adequate for your use. You will need one for mixing oil colours together and you can also use it, instead of a brush, for applying any kind of thick paint to paper and cardboard (powder, gouache, acrylic and oil).

Adhesives

There is a vast range of glues available. Useful ones are:

Cow gum/rubber cement

A rubber-based glue which is excellent for paper collage, mounting drawings and photographs. Adhesion is not immediate so pieces can be moved and rearranged. Any excess glue round the edges can be rubbed away or peeled off when dry like india rubber.

P.v.a.

This has a variety of trade names but is basically a strong, water-soluble, plastic adhesive that will stick almost anything. It is particularly useful for making three-dimensional constructions and sticking solid objects to a background. Diluted it can be used as a paper adhesive but once stuck the pieces cannot be removed. Art suppliers will give you a leaflet with further details.

I have given you a list of materials that can be bought from an art shop but these are not the only ones that can be used. All kinds of bits and pieces, scraps of paper, fabric and general waste material may be just what you need for a particular piece of work, notably when you are assembling collages.

Collage is a word derived from the French *coller*, to stick. It describes the method of constructing pictures by pasting together various kinds of papers. If you have not already tried this method, you will find it very enjoyable and there are many opportunities of using it in this book. Any paper, photographs, or even fabrics, can be used. I suggest you keep a 'collage box' and collect colour magazines, wall-paper sample books, old wrappings, patterned papers, odd bits and pieces from waste-paper baskets, and anything else that you happen to see.

Portfolio

Drawings and paintings need to be kept flat. Rolling them spoils the surface of the paper and they can never be satisfactorily flattened afterwards. Two large pieces of thick cardboard can be used but a portfolio with flaps is preferable as this can be more easily carried about from place to place.

Aim to keep all the work that you do. Often you will be tempted to screw it up and throw it away if you feel that you have not succeeded in doing just what you expected, yet it is always best to wait and look with fresh eyes at a later date, when you may feel differently about it. In any case, looking back, you can learn from your mistakes as much as from the work that pleases you.

Sketchbook

You have a notebook for each of your school subjects. Now you need a sketchbook as well. A sketchbook is really a 'visual notebook' to be used for recording information through your own drawings. Looking around with the eye of an *investigator* you will discover all kinds of interesting facts. Sometimes a quick diagram is all that is needed but at other times you may want your sketchbook for making detailed studies and for trying out new ideas.

Any notebook with a firm back and plain white paper will do but it needs to be a convenient size for carrying in a bag or pocket when you are drawing outside.

Each day you probably write several pages of words. Aim to fill one page of your sketchbook as well. Getting started is always difficult, especially when you have a new, empty book. Try out ideas from the following sections and the book will come alive with your own work.

Scrapbook

As well as a notebook for drawings, you will need a scrapbook in which you can paste photographs and other interesting cuttings that you find. You can buy one from a local stationer's shop or you can make your own by folding some sheets of paper in half and stitching them down the middle. Another method is to keep a loose-leaf scrapbook; pictures can be pasted on separate pieces of paper which are kept in a folder. Browse through some old magazines when you have read the next sections and see if you can collect appropriate pictures to illustrate the different headings.

Right
Drawing a plant (see page 92) and looking at a building (see page 80).

Opposite
Black pen and ink lines describe some of the intricate architectural details on the front of this Victorian station. (17)

1 Art is a language

Words are our familiar language. Through writing and speaking we tell others about our ideas and feelings. Yet we have other languages which serve special purposes like mathematics, music and art. The language of art consists of *line, shape, colour, texture, pattern* and *form*. These work together like words, and make visual 'sentences'. Just as we learn to choose from many words exactly those we need for what we want to say in our everyday language so we can learn to do the same using a visual language.

We have a lot of practice in sorting out our ideas and putting them down in words. Talking and writing forces us to express an idea in a positive way. The same is true in drawing. We look at something and need to think what we want to say about it. In other words, we must *select* what is of particular interest to us.

For instance, if you look at a tree you may be overwhelmed by its complexity. 'I can't possibly draw that.' you might say. Of course you can't draw every detail. Whatever you do will be a *translation* of the tree on to a flat piece of paper. The tree becomes a drawing. The drawing doesn't become a tree. The important thing is to look and begin to analyse what you can see.

Opposite
Elizabeth Haynes : Picture.
Early C18 embroidery in silk on canvas, 12½ × 14in, Victoria and Albert Museum, London.
To make this 'visual statement' the artist has selected three positive viewpoints and combined them together. The house is seen from the front, the garden is shown like an architect's plan, and the leaves on the oak tree are in close-up.

Right
Leonardo da Vinci : Study of a Tree.
1503, pen and ink over black chalk on blue paper, 26 × 39in, Royal Library, Windsor Castle. Courtesy of H.M. The Queen.
This drawing brings us in closer contact with the three-dimensional quality of a tree. The artist is observing the solid trunk and branches and the rough knobbly character of the bark.

At first you may be most aware of the thick solid trunk with branches subdividing again and again until they become the slender *lines* of twigs. In the winter we can see these lines, and their changes of direction quite clearly. They make up the total tree *shape* so that even without the leaves it is possible to identify a chestnut or a poplar or an oak. From a distance the branches form an intricate *pattern* against the sky. In the summer, these lines support a new pattern of overlapping leaf shapes making a mosaic of changing *colours.*

These are all *visual* qualities that we enjoy at a distance. You could also go right up to a tree and feel the *texture* of the trunk with its rough scratchy bark and look even more

closely at the tiny world of lines and shapes which combine together to give the trunks of trees their individual characters.

Now, having looked at your tree, you will need to choose which aspect you find most interesting and select appropriate materials for your study. You could study the *structure* of the trunk and branches, using soft lines of charcoal on sugar paper, or firmer lines of pen on cartridge paper. A different approach would be to make a pencil study of a really close-up portion of the bark. From further away, you could use paint to study the colour of the tree in relation to its surroundings.

Besides all these things you must decide on a size for the tree. Remember that you are 'translating' from the real tree into a new material. It will become a charcoal or a pen and ink tree, or a pencil or a paint tree. You may even combine some of these materials together. Try to relate the size of the paper to the material chosen. Charcoal makes soft broad marks and needs a large piece of paper. A pen makes fine lines and therefore a smaller size of paper would be appropriate.

When you begin drawing, you must concentrate and observe as intently as you can. Your eyes are not used to looking in this way. Usually a casual glance tells us the identity of an object and that is enough. Drawing can reveal the world to us in a completely new way. You will discover things that are not seen at first sight. Get into the habit of asking yourself questions while you are drawing. For instance, why do the edges of the tree seem to disappear into the surroundings, or perhaps, why do the edges stand out clearly? Why do you see some leaves more clearly than others? What do you think makes the different textures on the bark? When you have finished a friend may say: 'That doesn't look like that tree!' It may not be like the tree he has seen through his eyes, but you have seen something for yourself, and it has, in a way, become 'your' tree.

In the following section you will find suggestions for lots of other things to do. They will help you to explore some of the basic elements of the language of art. At first you can try these separately, as you might play some notes on a single musical instrument. But of course, when you listen to music you usually hear several instruments playing—and when you look at a work of art, you may see all the basic elements combined together.

Above
Piet Mondrian : Grey Tree.
1912, oil on canvas, 30 × 42in, Haags Gemeentemuseum.
Mondrian is concerned with analysing the structure of a bare
winter tree. Deliberately ignoring a mass of tiny details he searches
instead for the energetic rhythm of curving lines made by the
interweaving branches and the shape of the sky spaces in between.
Opposite
Van Gogh : Garden at St Remy.
1889, black crayon, pen and ink, 18 × 25in, Tate Gallery, London.
Van Gogh uses short, twisting, flame-like lines to express the
feeling of movement as the wind swirls through these trees.

Line

Line is the simplest and most direct way of expressing our ideas on paper. We use it all the time by bending and twisting it as it flows off the end of a pen or pencil to make writing; or if we want to show our ideas quickly and clearly by means of a diagram or plan. Line is a marvellous universal code. The strange thing is that although objects don't really have lines round them, we can use line as an equivalent for what we see, and everyone can read it and understand.

If you look around the room, you can begin to identify different kinds of lines. First look for lines that are fine and delicate and suggest the surface of the object. You can see the fur of your dog or cat as if it is made of tiny lines very close together; your jersey will have lines of stitches; a piece of furniture may show clearly the lines of wood graining. Next, look for strong, upright lines; perhaps the panelling of a radiator or the moulding round a window. Now look for the softer, undulating lines of the curtains and the clothes that you are wearing. Notice how all these different sorts of lines have different characters, and stand in contrast with each other: for instance, the curved, soft lines of a cat asleep on a chair which is made of straight, hard lines.

All these lines in the room link together to make up the view in front of you. As you move about and stand up and sit down, notice how the angles which the lines make with each other change. By observing these angles in drawing we can represent the effect of space and solidity on a flat surface. This is what is meant by 'perspective'. There is nothing alarming about it: you can find out all you need to know by looking carefully and training your eyes to follow these changes of angle as your viewpoint shifts. To guide and sharpen your observation, you can use a 'viewfinder'.

A viewfinder
This is a piece of card about 6 x 8in with a precise rectangle about 1 x 1½in cut out of the centre. Hold this up to frame what you are looking at and you will see how much easier it is to judge the angles of lines. Horizontal and vertical lines are the clearest. By comparing other lines with these, you will learn how to estimate their directions.

Through drawing you will discover much more about line which, like words, is one of our basic ways of communicating with each other.

It is interesting to look at the work of great artists to see some of the many ways in which line can be used. When you go to an art gallery or browse through books about art, look especially at drawings and notice how each artist has his own individual 'handwriting' or 'style'. But now you can make some lines of your own.

Opposite
Ben Nicholson: Rievaulx Abbey.
1954, pencil, 15 × 22in, Collection of Margaret Gardiner.
From a wealth of detail in this scene the artist has selected the most important shapes and chosen exactly the right lines to describe them. Compare the photograph with the drawing.

Below
Using a viewfinder.

All kinds of lines

cartridge paper/drawing paper
an assortment of drawing and painting materials
sketchbook

Each piece of writing that you do is made of your own personal lines curled into the shapes of letters. You know how different materials affect the look of this line. A soft pencil makes a different quality of line from a hard one, as does a ball-point from a wide-nib fountain pen. Chalks, crayons, paint, felt-tips—all have their own characteristics and it is worth finding out what these are.

Collect together as many different drawing materials as you can find and spread them round you. Choose a large sheet of cartridge paper and you are ready to begin. If you make all the lines either horizontal or vertical, it will be easier to compare them across the page.

1 Begin with a coloured crayon and draw several lines using different pressures. This will give you qualities of thinness and thickness. Try out other drawing tools and aim to get as much variety as possible.
2 Mix up some paint with only a little water and using a dry bristle brush, make several lines. Add more water to thin the paint, draw lines and compare these with the lines made with dryer paint.
3 Lines can be made with all kinds of other tools besides brushes. Dip a piece of card into the paint and make lines with this. Experiment with matchsticks, nails, string, twigs and anything else that you can think of.
4 You probably still have gaps on your paper. Fill these with lines that you feel suggest contrasting qualities like *softness*, *hardness*, *squashiness* and *prickliness*.

Look around you and you will see all kinds of lines in your own surroundings. On page 20, we thought about the lines made by overlapping branches of trees in winter. Next time you go out, look at trees and also look down at all the different cracks and joining lines of the pavement. Which materials do you think would be appropriate for drawing these lines?

Forty lines with different characters. Compare them with the lines that you make.

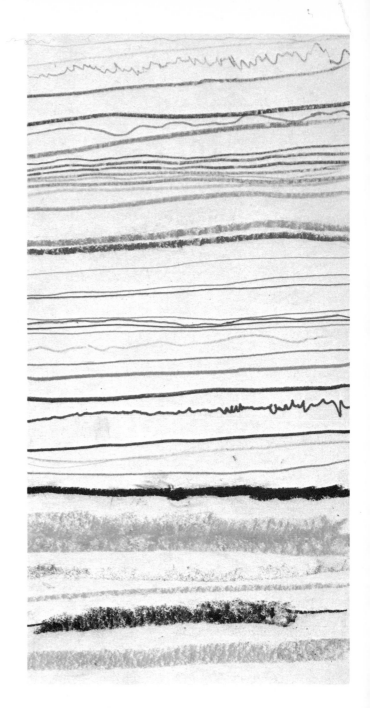

This picture of overlapping leaves was made by using powder paint and drawing directly with a brush. Notice the variety of lines. (11)

Lines on a surface

sketchbook or cartridge paper/drawing paper
ball-point or any drawing pen
magnifying glass

You may not be able to go out and study the lines of the pavement but you can easily look closely at your own hand. Spread out your fingers and look at the palm. Here you will see how the surface of your skin is made up of myriads of lines, some thick, some thin, and others branching out and overlapping. Look at the whorls on your finger tips. Can you see that they resemble contour lines on a map? In fact, you could think of your whole hand as a kind of map.

1 Using a pen, draw the outline of your hand. Make it life-size or larger.
2 Now use the pen to draw the lines of your skin. Look intently and try to record the *directions* of the main lines and the lines which grow out from these. Notice the thin delicate lines running between the thicker ones. Obviously you cannot draw every line but select those which seem to be most important in forming the character of your hand. If you have a magnifying glass you will find that this is fascinating to use and it will help you to observe carefully.
3 Unlike the lines of your skin, the lines that make up your hair can be picked up separately and moved about into a variety of positions. Look in a mirror at your own hair or ask a friend to sit so that you can study the back of his head. Notice how the total *shape* of the hair is made by the direction and rhythm of the lines as they grow out of the scalp. Using a pen or other materials, make a study of these lines.

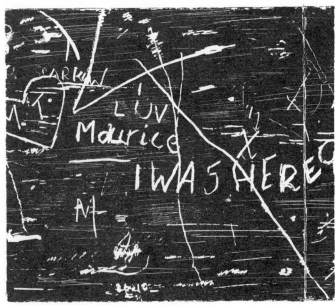

Take a line for a walk

any materials
paper about 12 x 8in, or sketchbook

By experimenting with different kinds of materials, you have discovered lines with all kinds of different characters. You know that lines can be curled into writing and you have seen how they represent the surface of skin and hair. Now you are going to take a line on a different path to see what happens.

1 To make your line, choose a material that you haven't used yet. It could be a fat wax crayon, an oil pastel or a piece of charcoal. The line will naturally be concerned with the surface that it walks on, so decide on a suitable paper for the material you have chosen.
2 Imagine that the line is only allowed to walk along horizontal or vertical paths. It can only change direction at right angles and it must never take its feet off the surface of the paper although it is allowed to cross over itself.
3 Begin from one side of the paper and go on walking, with your line, until you feel that it has made an interesting arrangement of squares and rectangles.

This time, your line has been used to construct an abstract design. The arrangement of shapes may be well-balanced and *symmetrical*, or some shapes may be clustered together in one corner, giving us a feeling of *asymmetry*. Which of these two feelings do you have when you look at your design?

Try this again on another piece of paper and see if you can make a design with a different feeling of balance.

Opposite top
Lines on the palm of a hand. Pen and black ink. (13)

Opposite bottom
A study of lines on the wooden surface of a desk. Wax engraving. (13)

Left
A line on an interesting walk. Can you find the starting point? Black felt-tip pen on white paper. (12)

Right
A simple pen line wraps round these objects and describes their shapes seen from two viewpoints. (17)

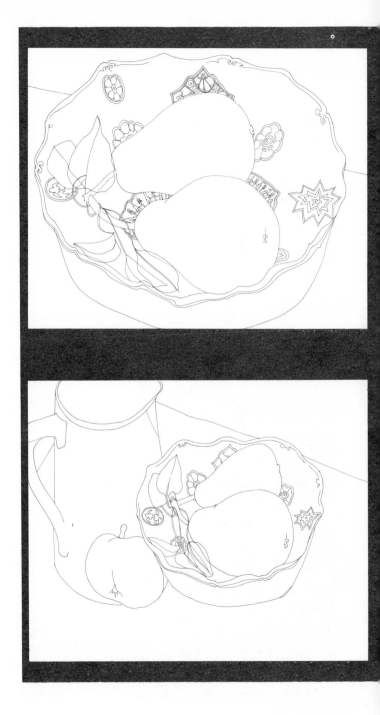

Drawing with string

a ball of string
p.v.a. glue
thick card or hardboard

Another line that can be used for drawing is a ready-made continuous line. Unwind a length from a ball of string. This line will make a drawing that looks quite different from the others you have made. Even more than pens, pencils, crayons and brushes string has characteristics which will limit what can be done. Invent a design which will be appropriate to the material.

1 You will need a firm background of thick card or hardboard. Cover this with a thin layer of p.v.a. glue.
2 Press one end of the string down firmly and then use the line to fill the board with a tightly packed decorative pattern. Do as much as possible using a continuous line. When necessary, cut the string and begin again. Go on adding more lines until the whole board is completely filled.

You may like to experiment with constructing an abstract design, a landscape or a portrait.

Line makes shapes

black paper about 12 x 16in
white paper about 12 x 16in
white crayons
black ball-point or fountain pen
black felt-tip or black ink and dip pen

In taking a line for a walk and drawing with string you have seen how lines join together to make *shapes.* This is another way of describing what happens when you make drawings. When you look at an object, you can leave out texture, tone and colour and choose a line to describe the shape. Here are two methods of drawing which show this clearly.

1 Take off your shoes and draw them, about life-size. Use a white crayon on black paper and look carefully to see the shapes between the lines. Try to choose lines to describe how the shoes have been constructed.

Opposite
Queen. String glued to hardboard. (17)

Right
Section through a cabbage. Pen and ink. (13)

Above
Self-portraits. Fine black felt-tip pen. 11½ x 16½in. See page 100. (11)

2 Make a black line-drawing on white paper, using pen and ink, a felt-tip or a ball-point pen. A bicycle is made up of all kinds of lines and is a fascinating object to draw in this way.

Look around and choose other familiar objects to draw in line, and add them to your notebook, e.g. hats, gloves, plants and other natural forms.

Drawing in line will help your eyes to stand still and look intently. Try to see the *shapes* of the spaces *between* the lines that you draw. Change your mind; draw other lines if you think you have judged badly. Don't worry about whether your drawing begins to look messy. The important thing is that your lines should help you to discover shapes and *not* to invent them.

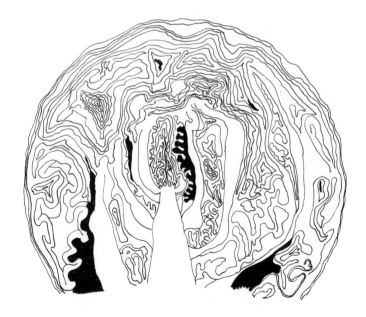

Line makes a jigsaw

sketchbook
viewfinder
drawing materials and paper

All around us, all the time, lines are taking a variety of different paths. Make a drawing to find just how good your eyes are at following directions.

Look for a group of objects on a table: some which just happen to be there, like plates and glasses on the dining-table or in the kitchen, or any surface littered with books and papers. Here you have a great assortment of lines, and your job is to find their directions. Verticals and horizontals are clear but other angles have to be judged carefully.

Use your viewfinder (page 22). Look through it to find a group of interesting lines and shapes that you would like to draw.

Decide if you want to work in your sketchbook or on a larger scale. The size of your paper should be the same proportion as the rectangle in the viewfinder. If necessary cut your viewfinder to a new proportion to fit your paper.

Choose appropriate paper and drawing materials to go together. Your first choice will probably be a pencil, which feels 'safe' because you can rub out mistakes. Try to find enough courage to put your rubber away. Drawing shows how we are thinking, and your line will be much more alive and less stodgy if you know you are aiming to get it right first time, rather than after a series of half-hearted attempts. One alternative to pencil would be charcoal, used on a large sheet of sugar paper/construction paper.

When you have chosen your materials, you are ready to begin. Look through the viewfinder again and try to see the *directions* of the lines. Notice how the *shapes* fit like a jigsaw into the aperture. It is quite a good idea to continue your drawing lines right through the objects as though you have X-ray eyes. This will help you to see how much the objects overlap each other. You will need to make adjustments but let your first lines remain, so that when you have finished your drawing will be a proper record of your exploration.

As with the fruit bowl and shoe drawings watch that the spaces *between* the lines do not turn out to be the wrong shape and thus make your whole drawing look inaccurate. The best advice is to remember that your draw-

Using a viewfinder to study the lines made by the branches of a tree. Notice how the shapes fit like a jigsaw into the aperture. Charcoal and white chalk on sugar paper/construction paper. (16)

ing is about that *particular* arrangement of *lines* and shapes at that *particular* moment—you will never see that group of objects or that person in exactly the same position again. Aim to discover the balance of the lines and shapes as you see them *now*.

Later we will look at other ways of using line. Lines can also be engraved into wax (page 85), cut in lino (page 131) and made to hang in space (page 141).

Shape

When drawing a group of objects you can see how *lines* can be used to explore the relationship of *shapes.* Certainly one shape can never exist in isolation, there is always another touching it. Even a single circle drawn within a rectangle of paper makes a second shape. Try it and see.

At first our eyes tend to identify objects separately without relating them to each other. Drawing helps our eyes to see that, in fact, each object is a shape linked on all sides to other shapes, part of a tightly packed jigsaw which surrounds us wherever we look.

While some shapes, like windows and bricks in a building, remain constant, others shift and change. Clouds can grow larger or smaller before our eyes. Each time a person moves, his shape changes in relationship to his surroundings. But there are other shapes which do not represent people and objects. These are geometric shapes like circles and squares which combined together make an endless variety of abstract patterns.

Yet another way in which we see shape is as a symbol. Certain combinations of shapes and colours make us think at once of a national flag, or a particular football team. The symbol may be a part of a universal code which communicates immediately, like a star or sun shape, or it may be derived from a natural form which has been translated into a flat 'heraldic' shape. All the complex natural details are eliminated in favour of a carefully selected *silhouette* which sums up the essence of the original object.

You see that shapes fulfil all kinds of purposes. They reveal the structure of the world around us and we can organize them together to make pictures, patterns and symbols.

We have have been thinking about shape as being flat and two-dimensional. There are, of course, solid three-dimensional shapes which we will look at in the section concerned with *form.*

Above
Parts of the inside of a clock. The shapes were cut from black card and glued on to a white background. This makes a raised surface from which rubbings can be taken. (14)

The shapes of objects can be seen more clearly when they are cut out of paper. Look at the shapes of the *spaces between* these objects. Collage on sugar paper/construction paper. (13)

31

Silhouettes and overlaps

cartridge paper/drawing paper
coloured felt-tips, ball-points or crayons

You can begin by picking up *shapes.* Take out the contents of your pocket, pencil-case, or bag, and spread them on the table.

1 Now choose an object, put it down on a piece of paper and draw round it using a coloured pen or crayon.
2 Pick up a different shape, put it on your paper and draw round it using another colour. Place the objects where you like, either separate, touching or overlapping. Notice that some have silhouettes with clear, hard edges while others, like crumpled handkerchiefs and paper tissues, have softer edges.
3 Turn the paper round into a new position: go on adding more objects until you feel that the design is full enough. Look at the shape of your paper, the shapes made by the objects and the shapes made *between* the objects.
4 Choose some of the shapes in the design and emphasize them by filling in with colours.

Most of the objects around us are either too large or too solid to be picked up, but when you are drawing you will find it helpful if you try to *imagine* that you *can* draw round them.

Cut-out shapes

four sheets of different coloured papers
large sheet of black paper
sharp scissors
cow gum/rubber cement

The materials that we use give their own special character to the shapes that we make. As a contrast to shapes made with *line* try using scissors and paper. Shapes cut with scissors have clear, crisp edges which make a strong silhouette. Try this for yourself.

Have the courage to cut directly without relying on timid pencil guide lines. At first you may find this difficult but if you concentrate and *feel* the shapes you are going to cut you will find that you can 'draw' with the scissors. Use a medium-size or large pair of scissors; small scissors are less easy to cut with.

1 Put a large sheet of black paper on the floor so that you can look down on what you are doing.
2 Using four sheets of different coloured papers cut out several large silhouette shapes of leaves, flowers and fruit.
3 Arrange these close together on the black paper without overlapping. This will allow you to observe the silhouette of each shape clearly and the new shapes made by the black paper in between. Move the pieces about and watch how these *black* shapes change.
4 Aim to arrive at a well-balanced arrangement of *both* the black and coloured shapes before sticking everything down with cow gum.

This feeling of balance is difficult to describe in words: it is something which you will learn to judge through your own experience of shapes, forms and colours. Some combinations of these elements produce only a dull static design while others produce a positive energy which makes the painting or any work of art come alive. This is a secret which you will discover for yourself. As a writer listens to words and a musician to sounds so we need to be alert to the silence of shapes and the other elements of the language of art which speak to us in their own way.

Above left
Contents of a bag. Each object has its own particular shape which is emphasized by drawing round it. Pencil on white paper. (11)

communicate a meaning without any need for words.

You yourself could try this problem by designing your own symbol. You could invent a family 'coat of arms', a club badge, or a design for the front of a T-shirt.

1 Draw the outline of a shield or a badge and divide it into two or more sections.
2 Choose the symbols that you want to use. You could combine an animal, bird or plant with an arrangement of geometric shapes like triangles, stripes and circles.
3 Each of your symbols must be designed to fit as a snug shape into its chosen section. The easiest way to solve this is by drawing the shapes with scissors. We have already seen how this method helps to reduce a complicated natural form into a simple flat shape.
4 Put the cut-out shape into its compartment and notice the new shapes appearing *behind it*. Aim to get a feeling of balance between the cut-out shape and these background shapes. Adjust the design by adding or cutting away more paper.
5 When you are satisfied with the arrangement, either stick the paper shapes down or draw round them and paint the sections using gouache or coloured inks.

Left
Fruit and leaves. Cut out coloured shapes against a black background. (16)

Below
A dragon symbol cut out of black paper and designed to fit snugly into an octagonal 'box'. (12)

Signs and symbols

coloured papers
scissors
sable brush
gouache
coloured inks

Footballers and jockeys wear clearly defined colours and shapes so that they can be identified at a glance. Flags and coats of arms are designed with the same purpose. A book on heraldry will show you examples. Modern examples of heraldic tradition are the signs used as trademarks to distinguish different products and companies. To be effective the shapes used in these designs must

Above
Georges Braque: Guitar, Jug and Fruit. © ADAGP Paris 1984.
1927, oil on canvas, 29 × 36in, Collection of Mr and Mrs
Lincoln Schuster, New York.
Notice how both the objects and the shapes between them are
equally important in this carefully organized design. The artist
has chosen to combine several viewpoints together: the shapes
of some objects being seen from above while others are shown
in profile.

Opposite right
The shapes of letters and the shapes made between the letters.
Gouache on cartridge paper. (13)

1 Look for the front page of a newspaper with some really large capital letters.
2 Cut an aperture 1½ × 1½in out of a piece of black paper and move this about on top of the newspaper until it frames an interesting arrangement of shapes. You are not looking for a whole word, but a close-up detail that shows the shape between the letters.
3 Stick the aperture down with sellotape. Draw a square, 4in or larger, on a piece of cartridge paper, and enlarge the shapes contained in the small square on to this. Although this may sound easy, you will find that you have to look hard if you are going to be accurate.
4 Colour the shapes you have found.

You can see that the shapes between letters are just as important as the shapes between objects.

Shapes in a picture

cartridge paper/drawing paper
tracing paper
pencil
gouache or crayons
sable brush

In this section we have been trying to use our eyes to focus on *shape.* Of course, every picture that we see is concerned with a particular arrangement of shapes. Often we are too interested in the subject, or the details, to notice, but the structure of the shapes is there holding the picture together and giving it a special individual character. You can prove this for yourself.

1 Choose a postcard reproduction of a painting that you like. Make a tracing which only includes the most important shapes. Leave out all the details, patterns and textures; look only for *shapes.*
2 Trace these shapes on to a piece of cartridge paper and paint or crayon them so as to make a completely flat arrangement of colours. You can choose colours relating to the original design or you may prefer to invent your own.
3 Now trace the shapes again and this time choose completely different colours. Try to watch how the colours

Word shapes

black paper about 6 x 6in
cartridge paper/drawing paper about 6 x 6in
gouache
sable brush
sellotape/Scotch tape

A newspaper headline, the destination of a bus, a brand name, what you are reading now: all this information is given to you through the shapes of letters. Our eyes are so well-trained to read meaning into the letters that we find it difficult to see the shapes. Try this experiment:

which you use affect the way in which we see the shapes. For instance, if you put an orange shape next to a blue shape the first time, the mood will be changed if, next time, you colour the same shapes purple and yellow, or grey and beige. Try out more schemes or trace other pictures in the same way, and try out more schemes on them. Now we are going to look at colour in more detail.

Above

The shapes in this postcard reproduction of a Toulouse-Lautrec have been emphasized by making a tracing which leaves out all the details. Repeating the design in this way helps us to appreciate the harmonious balance of shape and tone. (14)

Right

Compare these three designs. Although the same shapes have been repeated in each panel, they appear different because each one has been painted in a different colour scheme. (15)

Colour

Colour is your eyes in the mirror, your face, your clothes. It is other people in the room, the walls, the floor, the view from the window. Wherever we look colour looks back at us. We respond to it so strongly that we use it to describe our feelings: 'I saw red', he was 'blue with cold', 'green with jealousy' or 'white with anger'. In the theatre the director sets the stage and lights it according to the mood he wants to create in the audience. The colour of the witches in Shakespeare's *Macbeth* can be changed from green to purple to orange by the flick of a switch.

Nature changes colour before our eyes. Look at a patch of grass in strong sunlight and then the same grass in shadow. When you look at a landscape notice how quickly the colour changes as a cloud moves across the sun. The underlying structure of the landscape remains the same but the colour of the trees, fields and sky is constantly changing, first with the morning light, then in the strong light of midday, and finally evening and night.

Nature also changes colour with the seasons and slowly over many years. These colours that have grown with time are some of the most beautiful to look at. Look for tree trunks where moss is gradually changing the pinky brown of the bark to a warm olive green and look for walls where bricks have been washed by rain and weather until they each have their own beautiful colour quality. You will find things lying washed up on the beach that have been transformed by the action of waves and salt water. An ordinary petrol-can loses its mass-produced look by being dented and twisted into a new shape and it grows new colours through the action of sea and rust. See what other things you can find like this. They are individual pieces in a world of increasing uniformity.

In painting, colour makes us have an immediate feeling about the picture and establishes a particular mood. Which colours would you choose for a wet, cold, Monday-morning feeling and which would you choose for a warm, happy holiday feeling? Besides finding the mood of colour, you have to choose materials that will give the right *quality* of colour. For instance, felt-tip pens make vivid glowing colours, powder paints make matt, opaque colours, and watercolour gentle transparent tones.

As we have already seen, shapes cannot live separately and neither can colours. Look at any colour in the room and you will see another colour next to it. A brilliant red next to a bright green will have a different character from the same red next to a dark brown. With some pieces of coloured paper you could try this out for yourself.

We discover these things about colour, not only in making pictures, but when we choose clothes and objects to make our own environment. Clothes may be chosen for their pattern, and the texture of the fabric, but most of all for their colour. You may have had the chance to choose furnishings for your own room. The first thought was probably about which colours to put together. This will have shown you the difficulty of trying to imagine how the tiny sample in the paint catalogue will look when it is enlarged and painted all over a wall. Proportion affects colour. We feel differently about six square yards of blue emulsion on a wall from how we feel when we see the same blue on a postage stamp.

Light affects colour. The blue paint looks different on a sunny wall from how it looks on a wall in shadow. Texture affects colour. If you are choosing materials for curtains or a divan cover, you will find that a rough material like hessian will make red feel an altogether different colour from a similar red in shiny nylon.

You can see what an active visual force colour is; we are always surrounded by it in various shapes and textures. Colours link together to affect our moods and feelings. Our imagination fills with colour when we remember places we have visited and people that we know.

The following section suggests ways in which you can find out more about colour through your own painting.

Primary colours

vermilion	warm, orangey *red*
crimson	cool, pinky *red*
chrome	warm, golden *yellow*
ochre	cool, sandy *yellow*
ultramarine	warm, rich, dark *blue*
cobalt	cool, chalky, pale *blue*

A good way to identify these and to find out their characteristics is to make a colour 'patchwork'. On a piece of cartridge paper, rule an 18in square and divide it into 2in squares. Using either gouache or powder paint, fill six with each of the basic colours. Wherever squares meet edge to edge, make the colours *touch*, so that you see the full value of the *contrast* between them.

Do use plenty of paint when you are mixing colours. You should be able to *feel* it on the end of your brush and in your palette like thick cream. A little paint with a lot of water will never give you this enjoyment and will result in thin, washy colours without richness.

Secondary colours
These are the colours made by mixing two of the *primaries* together.

Red and blue = *purple*
Yellow and red = *orange*
Blue and yellow = *green*

Ultramarine and *chrome* make quite a different green from *cobalt* and *chrome*. Try it and see. Use all the combinations of two colours that you find : paint them into squares and compare them with each other.

Tertiary colours
These are the colours made by mixing two of the *secondaries* together.

Purple and orange
Orange and green
Green and purple

Mix a pair together and see what happens. Obviously the result will depend on which colours were used to make the secondary colours and the *proportion* of purple to orange and so on. Paint these into your patchwork.

A colour patchwork

cartridge paper/drawing paper
gouache or powder paint

Colour provides us with an enormous vocabulary to choose from. First there are all the colours that you can buy in tubes from an art shop. Then there is the vast range of colours that can be mixed from these. I suggest that you begin by limiting yourself to black, white and two of each of the *primary* colours. These are *red, yellow* and *blue*— the pure colours that cannot be made from other pigments.

Hue, intensity, temperature, tone

So far I have only been referring to the *hue* of colour—that is, its quality of redness, blueness or brownness. There are several other important qualities.

Intensity

The strength and brilliance of a colour indicates its *intensity*. By adding any other colour to it, you feel that this intensity has been lost. For instance, paint a square of pure *vermilion* in one of the spaces. Add a small quantity of white and paint another square. Notice the change of intensity. Now wash your brush and add a small quantity of black to vermilion and look at this change. You could paint several squares in this way. Go on adding more white or more black until the original feeling of the vermilion completely disappears.

Temperature

This is the warmth or coolness of colours. A pure vermilion not only has *intensity* it also has a feeling of *warmth*. By adding white, the colour changes to pink and feels *cooler*.

These qualities affect the mood of a painting, and also the way in which colours appear to advance towards the front of a picture or to recede into the background. Looking at a distant view you will see how cool colours like greys and blues appear to recede while warmer, richer colours seem closer.

Above
The colours in this painting capture the feeling of early summer when the trees are coming into full leaf. A variety of greens and whites contrast with the rusty brown colours on the barn roof and the brick walls. (15)

Tone

This is the *depth* of a colour. Black and white are the two extremes of *tone.* One is the darkest and the other is the lightest tone. Some colours are dark and therefore close, in tone, to black; some are light and close to white, while others may be midway between the two.

You may find it helpful to imagine black as the bottom of a well and therefore 'depth' 10, and white as the top of the well and 'depth' 1. Colours between these two extremes could have numbers from 2 to 9. For instance, if you look around the room, a red cushion may be dark in tone and about 'depth' 8, the carpet may be a little lighter and about 'depth' 6 and a newspaper almost white, and therefore 'depth' 2.

This is only a rough guide but it will help you to see colour not only as bright or subdued, warm or cool, but also as having a *tone* or 'depth' value. By appreciating this, you will be able to see how the darkness or lightness of a colour affects the balance of shapes in a painting. When you next visit an art exhibition, buy a black and white reproduction and take it with you to look at the original. This will help you to see colour in terms of tone.

Note that colours act on each other more strongly where their *tone* is similar.

Above
In this painting the lightest tone has been used for the surface of the water. Notice that the tones gradually darken as the water gets deeper. So that the fish and plants can be seen, they are painted in darker tones against the light areas and lighter tones against the darker areas. (12)

Complementary colours

I have made a series of colour studies in painting, simply flowers, red poppies, blue cornflowers, and myosotis, white and rose roses, yellow chrysanthemums—seeking oppositions of blue with orange, red and green, yellow and violet. Trying to render intense colour and not a grey harmony.

Van Gogh

See what happens when you put each *primary* against the mixture of the other two.

Red against green (blue and yellow)
Yellow against *purple* (red and blue)
Blue against *orange* (yellow and red)

These are the colours that naturally co-exist with each other. You can see that they each have different *tone* values: *yellow* has the *lightest* tone while *purple* has the *darkest*. Therefore yellow needs the *smallest* area to reflect a given amount of light and purple needs the *largest* area. You can understand this if you imagine painting the walls of a kitchen—one yellow wall would reflect far more light than one purple wall.

It may help you to think that yellow needs 3 units of space to reflect a given amount of light, orange needs 4, red and green 6 each, blue needs 8, and purple needs three times as much as yellow—9 units. This guide will help you to see the relative amount of space that each complementary colour needs to occupy if it is to relate harmoniously with its opposite colour. You could experiment by trying some of these ideas out on another piece of paper.

Black and white

Black and white are also colours which have their own subdued beauty. There are many different kinds of black and white, just as there are many kinds of reds, yellows and blues.

Here is an experiment to try. You will need a piece of white paper and a piece of black paper. Look around for all the black and white things that you can see. Hold the pieces of paper up against them and compare them. A 'white' tablecloth, cupboard and plate will all be variations on your white paper. A 'black' jersey, shoe and frying pan, will all be variations on your black paper.

See what variations you can mix with paint. Theoretically by mixing all three *primaries* together you should achieve black, but, in fact, you will get a rich dark colour that varies according to the proportions of the primaries used. See how many 'blacks' you can make and add them to your patchwork of squares. Do the same thing with white.

On page 49 I have described a method for making a paper mosaic. For this, you would find it helpful to have some pieces of black and white paper. Mix up more colour than you need for a square and paint strips of paper as well. Make them about 10in long and 2in wide.

Discover new colours

I hope that you still have some empty squares in your colour patchwork. Here is a way of adding to it and discovering new colours at the same time.

1 Make a list of the names of all the paints that you have.
2 Cross two names off the list and mix these two colours together. Use plenty of paint so that you have enough to fill a square and leave some in your mixing palette.
3 Cross another name off the list and add this colour to the mixture in your palette. Fill a square with the new colour.
4 Continue in this way until no more names are left. Keep adding to the original mixture and if it becomes too dark, add white and continue.

In using this method you will meet strange, unusual colours which you may never have discovered in the normal way of mixing.

I have already stressed the importance of training your eyes to be selective when you are drawing. Whenever you use colour in any way, you must be equally selective. The whole orchestra of colour is far too unwieldy: you need to choose those colours which are appropriate for your purpose.

Cut a 2in square from the centre of a piece of paper and move it about over the colour patchwork. See if you can select colour groups that suggest particular moods and feelings. Which colours would combine to make a painting of a stormy sea or a scorched landscape? Which do

you think suggest feelings of discord, happiness, violence, and sadness? You can see how valuable it would be to choose colours in this positive way for your own paintings.

The days of the week each have their own particular character. Fill a piece of paper with seven colours which represent your own feelings about each day.

Concentrate on green

Another way of discovering new colours is by collecting together a group of objects of the same *hue*. Suppose you choose green: you could include a pimento, a cucumber, a jersey, a book, a jug, a towel—anything you like.

1 Put all the objects together on a table or on a low stool and look at them through your viewfinder.
2 Choose a key colour, i.e. one that feels important in the balance of colours that you can see. Mix a quantity of this colour and paint in the *shapes* that it occupies. Use any size of paper but keep it to the same proportions as your viewfinder. *Avoid* using line: paint the *shapes* directly.
   If you have a palette knife, you could mix the paint extra thickly and apply it with this instead of a brush.
3 Look at the colour *next* to the first colour you have chosen and try to mix this. Remember that colour does not live in isolation and you cannot judge whether the feeling of the colour is right until it actually *touches* the previous one. Go on building up colour and shape in this way. Don't worry about precise edges—enjoy the substance of the paint and the quality of the colour.

This will help you to appreciate the immense variety within the colours around us. You could try this idea using another colour as a starting point.

Above left
Unloading fish boxes.
Here black, white and grey is used to make a strong pattern of shapes. Black and white gouache on sugar paper. (15)

Left
The objects chosen for this painting were based on a scheme of grey, beige, and pale yellows. Although you cannot see the actual colours in this reproduction you can still appreciate the light and dark *tonal* pattern that these colours make. (13)

42

Pattern

Line, shape and colour can all contribute towards making *pattern*.

Any shape makes a pattern when it is repeated many times. Squares can become a chess-board, a sheet of graph paper, or a check fabric. Lines used together become stripes. Overlapping circles make a fish-scale pattern.

There are endless ways in which repeating shapes can be combined to make patterns. We can see this in all the ways in which man has used decoration throughout history. Richly tiled floors, painted ceilings, mosaics, pottery, illuminated manuscripts, printed fabrics, tapestries and carpets all demonstrate his delight in pattern.

You may have a local museum in your town where you can see a collection of folk art. This is the art of ordinary people who used to make things and decorate them for their own pleasure. You will see how the simplest decoration can enrich furniture, pottery, toys and other everyday things, and how traditional crafts, like weaving, smocking, lace-making, basketry, and embroidery each produce their own special patterns.

All these are examples of deliberate patterns. We often see others that happen unintentionally. Units assembled together for practical purposes are examples of this. For instance, crates of milk bottles, tiles on a roof, cups on a canteen counter, and cars packed closely together in a car park. This repetition of a single related shape again produces a feeling of pattern.

Nature provides us with an immense variety of patterns. These are not decorative but functional in purpose. Stripes on animals are patterns that work as camouflage: others use pattern as a means of attraction. Plants, fruit, vegetables and shells each have their own intricate pattern structures which are fascinating to study.

Many churches have large circular windows filled with stained glass. This design is based on one of these structures. The drawing was made on black paper and the shapes of the pattern cut out to make a stencil. This stencil was placed flat on to a piece of white paper and dilute paint blown through the apertures with a fixative spray. (12)

Structures

sketchbook
drawing materials

The best way to find out more about pattern is to look at the structure of natural forms. These are incredibly rich and varied. Usually we just glance at the markings on shells, plants, insects and animals, but by pausing and really *observing* them we can add a lot of ideas to our visual vocabulary.

1 Cut an orange and a tomato in half across the middle and compare the different patterns that you find. Make some simple *line* drawings in your sketchbook which will help you to investigate the structure of each fruit.
2 Cut an onion in half across the middle and cut a sprout or a cabbage in half vertically. Look at the concentric circles inside the onion and the tree-like branching structure of the sprout and cabbage. Make drawings of these.
3 Experiment with sections through other natural forms, e.g. pomegranates, pimentos, carrots and cucumbers, and make drawings of the patterns that you find.

Single units

thick card/poster board or hardboard
p.v.a. glue

You find other examples of pattern in many of the ordinary man-made things around you. Bricks in a wall, fences, vertical railings and packets on display in a supermarket, all these make different pattern structures based on a repetition of related shapes.

You yourself could experiment with making similar patterns. Collect a number of identical small objects that are easily available, e.g. matchsticks, metal bottle-tops, labels, tickets, stamps, polo-mints, drawing pins. You need enough to make an interesting repeat pattern of shapes when you arrange them together.

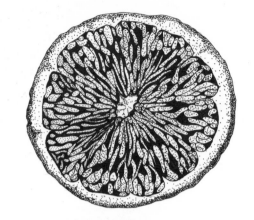

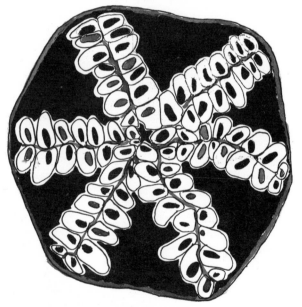

Above
Pattern revealed when an orange is cut in half. Pen and black ink. (16)
Section through a pomegranate. Brush and black ink. (13)

Opposite
Flat sponges from the tops of medicine bottles assembled together to make a pattern of circles. (16)

Pattern made by repeating the shapes of liquorice allsorts. Gouache on white card. (18)

Drawings were made of a staircase from several different points of view and, using methods of overlap and transparency, they were organised together into this fascinating complex design. Notice how warm and cool colours are used to suggest space and small areas of concentrated pattern contrast with the angular structures of the staircase. See page 90. Gouache on white paper. 20 × 25in. (18)

Top right
A sheet of paper was divided into an arrangement of varying sizes of squares and rectangles. The shapes were filled with both warm and cold colours mixed to explore a wide tonal range and make one area into a special 'focal point'. Can you find it? See page 38. (12)

Right
The 'colour patchwork' above formed the inspiration for this still life. Objects with similar colours, e.g. the red mug, green bottles, yellow tin and flower pot, were arranged together on a red and blue striped cloth. Although the 'patchwork' is two dimensional, this painting shows similar colours being used to describe space and three dimensions. Gouache on grey paper. 11 × 15in. (12)

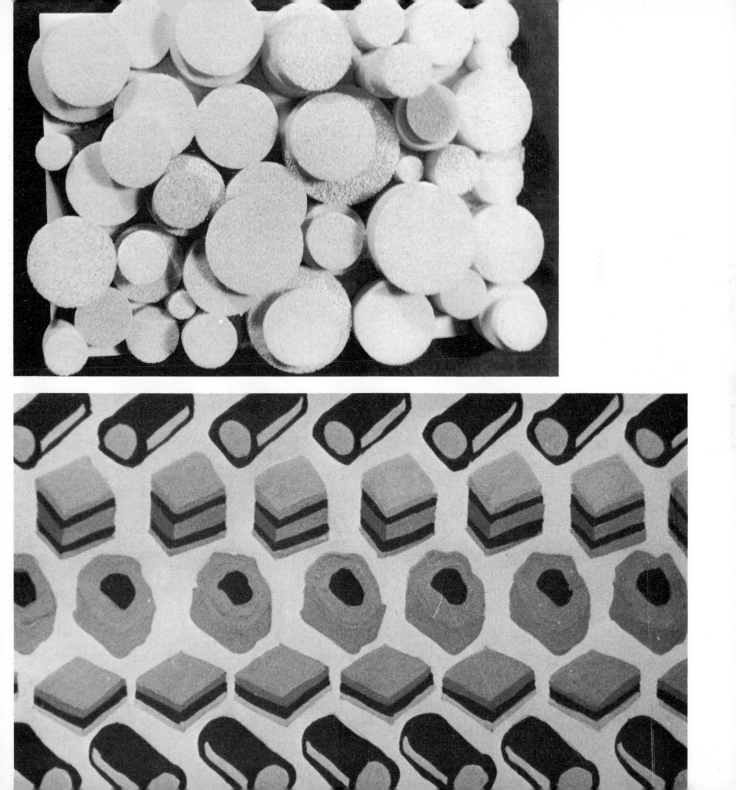

1 Put the bottle-tops or whatever you have collected on a piece of thick card or board and move them about until you arrive at an arrangement that makes the most interesting pattern.
2 Mark the positions and stick down with p.v.a. glue.

The bottle-tops make a pattern of *circles*. A pattern of smaller circles could be made by using various sizes of nail heads. Try hammering them closely together into a thick piece of wood and arrange them to make a pattern.

Experiment with arrangements of other shapes. Match-sticks will make patterns of vertical or horizontal *lines*; stamps or tickets will make patterns of *rectangles*.

Printed pattern

newsprint/sugar paper
powder colour
bristle brush
sharp kitchen knife
potato

Another way of using single units to make pattern is by printing. You may be wearing a patterned fabric or have a printed wallpaper or fabric in your room. If you look closely you will be able to see the units which have been repeated to make the design. Often these single units are remarkably simple and yet the overall effect of the pattern is rich and interesting.

Right
Design based on a potato cut in half horizontally. (12)
Here the potato has been cut into a rectangular block. Can you find the single unit which makes the design? (12)

Opposite
Persian manuscript.
C16, gold and mineral colours on paper, 7 × 12in, British Museum, London.
As in the overall design of a carpet, there is no feeling of space in this picture: the artist has organized a rich variety of patterns and shapes in a purely two-dimensional way.

Here is a printing method which will help you to discover this for yourself.

1 Cut up some sheets of newsprint or other absorbent paper into pieces 12 x 8in or larger.
2 Mix up some powder paint to make a darkish colour which will show up clearly against the paper. Keep a liquid consistency and make enough to fill a saucer.
3 Cut a potato in half horizontally. Use a really sharp knife. Brush paint across the surface and press the block down firmly on to the paper. Continue printing in this way until the whole page is completely covered with shapes that touch. Filling the paper is essential: it is no use judging an all-over pattern when only a few prints have been taken.
4 Now print another page and use a second block to overprint the first with a different colour.
5 Turn the block into a square by cutting off the curved edges. Experiment with this new block to find a variety of pattern arrangements. Notice how the shapes of the unprinted paper become part of the design.
6 Use a knife to remove one or two lines from the surface of the block and print another page.

By changing the shape, colour and arrangement of this single block you will be able to discover a wide variety of patterns. You could try a larger unit by using a swede or turnip in a similar way.

With this method you can make unusual wrapping papers and book covers and even decorate a corner of your room with your own wallpaper.

Counterchange

sketchbook or squared maths paper/graph paper
pencil
ruler
black felt-tip pen

A chess-board is a simple pattern of squares. Each black square has a white one touching it and each white square a black one touching it. This alternation of light and dark shapes is an example of a counterchange scheme. By using this scheme, you will discover lots of ways of elaborating simple patterns.

1 Use a piece of squared maths paper or fill a page of your sketchbook with a grid of squares, $\frac{1}{2}$ x $\frac{1}{2}$in.
2 With a fine black felt-tip pen, fill in a few squares to make a 'chess-board' counterchange pattern.
3 Now divide some squares across diagonally to make triangles. Fill in the shapes with a counterchange scheme, always a black shape next to a white and a white next to a black.
4 Think of other ways of dividing the squares with simple geometric shapes. Try circles and crosses. Fill them in with black and white in a similar way.
5 Experiment on another grid of squares, using two colours, one light and one dark.

Work out a cover design for one of your school notebooks. An old piece of furniture—a chest of drawers, chair or table—could also be brightened up by decorating with a painted counterchange design.

Mosaic

variations on black and white paper
grey sugar paper/construction paper
scissors
cow gum/rubber cement

You could use this idea of counterchanging tones to make a paper mosaic. First you need some sheets of black and white paper. Try to find a variety of blacks and whites. You may have tried mixing the variations on black and white suggested on page 41. These papers could be used.

You can make a paper mosaic of any size but begin with a square of paper about 20 x 20in.

1 Divide up the square into a simple geometric design with clear shapes.
2 Cut up your bands of black and white variations into small pieces about $\frac{1}{2}$ x $\frac{1}{2}$in. Keep each colour in a separate container.

Opposite
Experiments with counterchange patterns. (13)

Right
Mosaic made by counterchanging light and dark tones of paper.

Below right
Detail showing close arrangement of the pieces. (12)

3 Fill one shape with either light or dark pieces. Stick them down close together, without overlapping, so that almost all the background disappears.
4 The adjoining shape must be filled with the opposite *tone* so that the two shapes show clearly against each other. See page 48 for this.
5 Go on until the whole panel is covered. If other members of your family make their own panels, you could build up an attractive mural.
6 Experiment by making another design using brighter colours. You might also collect pebbles and broken pieces of china which can be set into a plaster or cement base. See page 111.

Playing cards

a pack of cards
white cardboard
gouache

Playing cards are splendid examples of shape and pattern combining together to make a totally satisfying design. Take the Kings, Queens and Jacks from the pack and spread them out. Look at the way each of the characters fits perfectly into his or her rectangular box, leaving just enough room for the symbol of the suit by the head. The royal clothes are shown as simple, stylized shapes, decorated with clear geometrical patterns. Red, yellow, blue, black and white are used in an ingenious way to make a rich variety of colour combinations.

See if you can design your own court cards. Choose either a King, Queen or Jack. Work to the same size or, if you like, larger. Draw a wide margin round the edge for the suit symbols.

1 Divide the rectangle in half. Try out a simple head, shoulders and crown and reverse your drawing for the lower half of the rectangle. Heads are either shown in profile or three-quarter view and are drawn in line. Notice how hands and objects are simplified to make a flat pattern.
2 Choose clear, geometric patterns to decorate the clothes, and paint with gouache to make a smooth matt surface. See colour facing page 96.

Texture

We have seen that our visual world is made up of lines, shapes, colours and patterns. It is also made of *textures*: that is surfaces which we appreciate through *touch* and *sight.*

If you think of a brick wall, a sandy beach or a furry animal, you can imagine how these surfaces would feel if you touched them. It would be difficult to explain these sensations in words but they play an important part in our visual language. The wall, the beach and the animal would be far less pleasing, both to look at and to touch, if they were all made of smooth plastic.

If the surface of an object feels inappropriate, it can be positively disturbing. Recently a manufacturer produced some cars with a suede surface instead of the usual polished metal. It was certainly eye-catching but very uncomfortable to look at. You may have seen the work of Claes Oldenberg, an American artist, who has experimented in a similar way by making giant, furry lollipops and squashy, deflatable typewriters.

Texture is an important element in the language of art. The materials that we use each have their own textural qualities. Pencil, charcoal, crayon, ink, watercolour and powder paint, all make different surfaces to look at, as we found in our experiments with line.

In looking at these materials we are able to enjoy texture through our sense of sight, though often we are remembering experience of touch. In looking at a photograph we do the same thing. Our experience enables us to look at a two-dimensional image and to translate it into texture.

The camera is also able to show us textures which are normally hidden from sight. Under immense magnification, a butterfly wing, a person's tongue, a frost crystal, and a moon crater all reveal amazing textural surfaces.

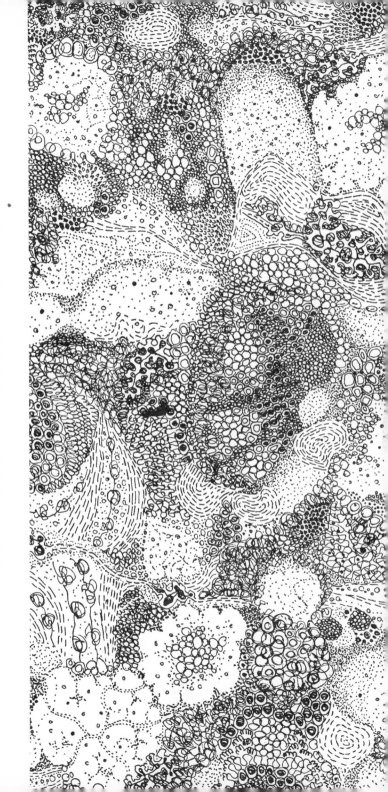

Pen and ink drawing based on the textures revealed when a patch of earth is magnified. (17)

Opposite
A group of people, bricks and lupin leaves each form patterns.

You may be able to see photographs like these in books at school or in your local library. And if you have an ordinary magnifying glass, you can re-examine the surface of familiar things—for example, a plank of wood, a towel, the carpet and a patch of gravel, etc.

This kind of close-up looking is a good way of training your eyes to pause and consider the subtleties of surfaces.

Paint and ink textures

various kinds of paper
paints and inks
turpentine

Here are some of the many ways in which you can make textures with paint and inks. You can experiment on any paper, including the backs of old drawings.

1 Mix up some very thick paint. Use a dry brush to cover a sheet of paper with the paint. Enjoy the texture of the brush lines.
2 Add more water to the paint in your palette. Fill your brush and let the paint dribble down on to a sheet of cartridge paper. Move your brush in all directions.
3 Load your brush with paint and shake it over another sheet of paper. Add a second colour with another brush. Then try this method using coloured inks.
4 Damp a sheet of paper with a wet sponge. Load your brush with liquid paint or ink and drop blobs of colour on to the damp paper. Watch the textures grow on the surface. To prevent the paper from buckling up, you could stretch it before you begin (see page 13).
5 Rub a candle or wax crayon firmly across a piece of paper. Liquid paint or coloured ink brushed over the top will retreat from the wax leaving a special texture.
6 Half fill a sink with water. Dilute some oil paint with turpentine and pour a little of the mixture on to the water. Agitate the surface gently so that the colour moves about. Put a piece of paper on to the water and leave for a few moments. Lift it up carefully and look at the textures you have made. See page 70.
7 Leave all the sheets of paper to dry. Press them flat between two boards and keep them ready to use for making paper collages where texture is needed.

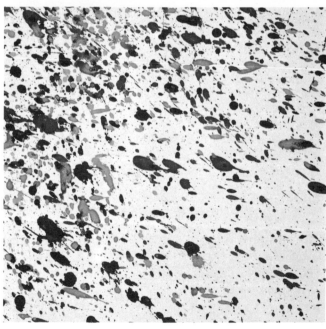

Opposite top
Textures made by using thick paint with a dry brush.

Opposite
Textures made by loading a brush with liquid paint and shaking
it over the paper.

Above
Jan van Eyck: detail from The Marriage of the Arnolfini.
1434, National Gallery, London.
The artist was interested in observing each different surface texture
in the room. In this detail you can see how he used his paint to
record the texture of the dog's fur contrasted with the wooden floor.

Line textures

black drawing ink
penholder with a fine nib or a fountain pen
sketchbook

Apart from the textures that can be made with paint, there are others that can be made with lines. Blobs of paint can suggest an equivalent for a patch of earth or wall, *lines* can be used to suggest an equivalent for furriness or grittiness. Experiment with pen lines and see what kind of textures you can make.

1 Collect some textured surfaces to look at; assorted fabrics, wool, tree bark, feathers, walnuts, shells, wood, pieces of rock, a pan scourer, sponge, brush, sandpaper.
2 Draw a block of 16 x 1in squares in your sketchbook.
3 Look very closely at one of the things in your collection. You will see the texture more clearly if you use a view-finder with a 1 x 1in square cut in the centre. Imagine

the lines that could suggest an equivalent for the texture of that surface. Try them out in one of your squares.
4 Choose another surface with a different texture and try again. Go on experimenting until all the squares are complete.

This method will help you to discover new ways of using your pen. It will be useful for drawings where you want to suggest textured surfaces.

Above
Chalks and sugar paper were the appropriate materials to choose to emphasize the soft qualities of this feather. (14)

Opposite above
Rubbing taken from a worn paving stone. White wax crayon on black paper.

Opposite below
Taking a rubbing.

Rubbings

any thin, strong paper
wax crayons
cobbler's 'heel-ball'
sellotape/Scotch tape

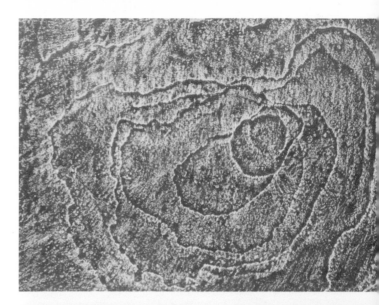

Another way of making textured papers is by taking rubbings of different surfaces. You will need some sheets of thin, strong paper, and a black wax crayon. If you can find a shoe-mender who will sell you a stick of cobbler's 'heel-ball', so much the better: this is a harder wax and makes a firmer image.

1 Hunt around for interesting surfaces to record. Begin with a piece of wood. Hold the paper down firmly and rub with the wax until you have made a strong dark texture.
2 Aim to collect a rich variety of contrasting textures. Look for rough walls, fences, floors, pavements, matting, basketwork, gratings, doors, fabrics, tree trunks, etc.
3 Cut small squares from each of the rubbings and stick into your scrapbook to make a page of textures. Add these textured papers to your collection for making collages.

Through making rubbings you will discover an amazing variety of textural surfaces which you may hardly have looked at before. This is another way of training your eyes to pause and look more intently.

Some churches have beautiful monumental brasses which can be recorded by this method of rubbing. You may see some in your local church or when you are away on holiday. Before you begin you must ask permission from the vicar and probably pay a small fee for the privilege.

Take with you a roll of decorator's lining paper, or 'shelf paper', which is usually available at a hardware store, or a roll of 'detail paper' from an art shop; the rest of the equipment listed above; something to kneel on and a soft duster.

1 Dust the brass with a soft cloth to remove any grit.
2 Unroll your paper so that it covers the brass *completely*.

Fasten the edges down securely with sellotape to prevent the paper moving and to make sure that no wax touches the brass or the stone surround.

3 Steady the paper with your hand and rub the wax gently but firmly across the surface. At first a greyish tone will appear; go on rubbing steadily in all directions until the lines show clearly against a really dark background. You may succeed in making a good rubbing from a small brass in about an hour but a larger one may take several hours so be prepared to settle down and persevere.

4 When you have finished, peel off the sellotape and roll up the paper. Make sure that you remove all your bits and pieces and leave everything exactly as you found it.

Some art shops sell special sticks of wax for this purpose and besides black you may be able to buy gold and silver. These metallic waxes look splendid used on black paper.

Above
Any raised surface makes an interesting rubbing. This one was taken from the top of a nineteenth-century iron combustion stove found in a church in Shropshire.

Collage

your own collection of textured papers
cow gum/rubber cement or p.v.a. glue
scissors

Look at the collection of papers you have made through paint textures and rubbings. You will have a mixture of light and dark tones, open and closed-up patterns, stripey, speckly and blobby textures. Use some of them to make a picture.

1 Choose a good subject to make in textured papers. You might like to invent a landscape or an imaginary city or a portrait of a woman wearing a fabulous hat or a man with an enormous beard.

2 Move your textured papers about and try out some ideas. Scissors will cut a shape with hard edges and your fingers will tear a shape with softer, broken edges. Choose the right edges for your subject. Do everything by cutting or tearing. Don't worry about pencil guide lines: they are not necessary.

3 When you have finished arranging the pieces, stick everything down with cow gum.

4 Pin your collage up. Stand back and look at it. Add more pieces if you think it is necessary.

On page 126 you can see how textured papers have been used to make people for a book, *Heads, Bodies and Legs.*

Above
Experiments with paint textures provided the papers used in
these collages. The soft, broken edges were made by tearing out
the shapes without using preliminary pencil lines. (11)

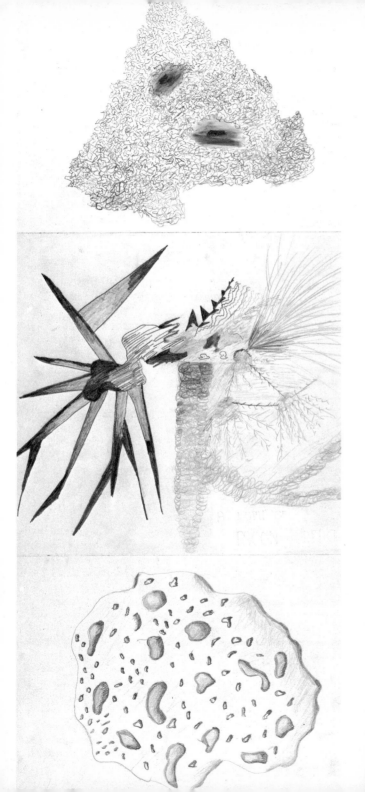

Surfaces

You have seen how paint, ink and wax can be used to suggest textures on paper; now see what you can do with a pencil. This is probably your most familiar tool which you use each day for writing notes and you may be unaware of the tonal and textural qualities it possesses when you use it for drawing.

Here is a way of exploring some of the possibilities.

1 Imagine that you are handling something unfamiliar—perhaps a piece of rock from the moon.
2 Make drawings to suggest ideas of what the rock *feels* like in your hands. Invent equivalents for sensations like squidginess, prickliness, etc. Explore the full range of tones from a rich, velvety black to a light grey and avoid using only one grey tone.

You can invent your own idea of moon substance or, if you like, refer to books that show photographs taken by the astronauts. Another interesting source of information are highly magnified photographs of organic structures.

Opposite
Photographs of textures. Can you identify them?

Below
Designs based on information taken from electron microscope photographs of organic structures. Gouache. (14)

Left
Pencil used to suggest textural qualities in 'moon substance'. (13)

Form

You walk into a room and a piece of air the shape of you is displaced; your three-dimensional *form* has pushed it out of the way. Add an armchair and a table and the same thing happens. Drop a heavy stone into wet mud and it makes a hole the size of its own shape. All three-dimensional things have volume and occupy *space*.

This is the element in the language of art which concerns the sculptor. He designs his work to live in space. We need to walk all round solid forms before we can say that we have seen them properly. We also feel that we want to reach out and touch them. Unfortunately in galleries and museums touching is not usually allowed. The only time that I have seen notices actually *asking* people to touch the sculptures was at the exhibitions of Henry Moore and Barbara Hepworth in the Tate Gallery, London. This certainly added to the enjoyment of their work.

Give a friend a three-dimensional object like a pebble or a shell, and watch how he turns it round in his hands and feels the surface with his fingers. Our sense of form is directly connected with this need to touch and handle.

Linked with this is our sense of space. Our landscapes are rather like gigantic sculptures in which we live and move about. You have probably felt a special pleasure in walking through woods or running across a vast empty beach. The space around us allows us to enjoy the *form* of the landscape—its three-dimensional quality.

Man-made constructions interrupt this form and space, changing landscapes into cities. Roads carve through hills, bridges span rivers and buildings grow up into the sky. Architects and town-planners have a great responsibility; their decisions affect our visual surroundings in a far more critical way than the work of any other designers. They have the problem of designing three-dimensionally in space, which means that they have to see how the solid mass of one building will relate to other buildings and to the landscape around. Within the buildings, the architect has to think about the individual spaces and try to relate the design of these to the people who will use them. The sensations we experience in a big echoing cathedral are different from those we feel in a crowded lift.

You can see that *form* is a very important part of our visual language. Every other element that we have looked at—*line, shape, colour, texture, pattern*—can all contribute to representing this three-dimensional quality of *form.* Look for interesting examples for your scrapbook. Collect photographs of sculpture, landscape and architecture and make your own drawings of smaller objects like pebbles, shells, gnarled wood and other natural forms. Henry Moore, who has studied the rhythms of natural forms more than any other sculptor, gives us a reminder:

The sensitive observer of sculpture must also learn to feel shape simply as shape, not as description or reminiscence. He must, for example, perceive an egg as a simple single solid shape, quite apart from its significance as food or from the literary idea that it will become a bird.

Above
Henry Moore : Recumbent figure.
1938, hornton stone, $35 \times 52\frac{1}{4} \times 29$in, Tate Gallery, London.
A stone carving in which the sculptor is exploring the human form as a great landscape structure of hills and cave-like hollows. He has said, 'A hole can have as much shape meaning as a solid form'.
Opposite
Barbara Hepworth : Three forms.
1935, marble, $7\frac{7}{8} \times 21 \times 13\frac{1}{2}$in, Tate Gallery, London.

Cubes, cylinders and spheres

grey sugar paper/construction paper
charcoal and white chalk
viewfinder

I have explained how necessary it is to observe intently when you are drawing, and how you must decide what you are going to investigate before you begin. In the previous sections you have found suggestions for ways in which you can discover more about two-dimensional *shapes, texture, pattern* and *colour.* Now we are going to think about how to emphasize the solid *form* of objects.

Collect a few things and put them on the table—a box, a tin, a bottle and a ball. Look at them through your viewfinder. Now what you see is very complicated. You could search for the *shapes* of the objects, using *line,* you could study the *textural* differences, or the relationship of of *colours.* Instead we are going to concentrate on what makes the objects look three-dimensional.

Do you see that each object has a surface that is facing you and surfaces that recede from you? Reach out and touch the objects and you can feel this for yourself. Each object also has a surface which is *facing the main source of light* and other surfaces which face in different directions and so receive less light. Look at the box. One side will be *light* in *tone* and the others *darker.* This change of tone from light to dark can be used in drawing to emphasize the solidity of objects. 'Shading' is probably the word that you know that describes this and it may suggest that there is some special kind of technique to be learnt. Forget about this. Shading is really just using pens, pencils, crayons and paints in any way that suits you to make light and dark tones.

Before you begin drawing, move the objects about until they are in a position where the source of light causes the maximum contrast of light and dark.

1 Using grey sugar paper, charcoal and white chalk, make a study of these changes of *tone*. Begin by lightly drawing the *shapes* of the objects.
2 Now observe the group through half-closed eyes—this will help you to see the tonal differences more clearly. Decide which are the *lightest* and which are the *darkest* tones and chalk in these areas first. You must

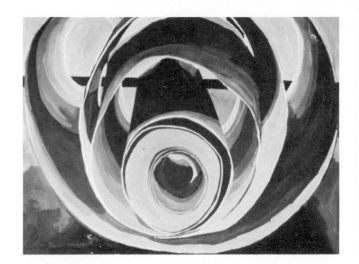

Top
A study exploring the three-dimensional quality of a roll of paper. Acrylic paint on white card. (18)

Above
Objects on a table. Notice how each object has one surface facing the main source of light. Charcoal and white chalk on grey sugar paper. (14)

Opposite
Ways of constructing solid forms. Pencil, pen, and paper collage. (18)

think while you are selecting these tones: sometimes light can cast strange shadows which flatten the form of the object instead of describing it. It is no use just copying tone, you must try to understand *why* one part of the object is darker than another. Imagine that you are looking at a miniature landscape or town in which you can walk about.

Leave out *line*, just work with blacks, whites and greys. Notice how a sharp edge, like the side of a box, makes a sharp change of tone, while a rounded form, like a tin, makes a more gradual change.

A good alternative to chalks would be powder paint or gouache limited to black and white. You need to use materials which will help you make tonal adjustments. Remember that it is far better to change your mind if necessary, and to leave your work with its mistakes even though you fear that it will begin to look messy. You will only learn to be a good investigator if you forget about aiming for a superficially tidy result.

change. You could experiment by shining a torch on to the paper and watch what happens.

2 Choose an interesting lighting position and make a close-up painting. Imagine that the paper has become a heavy piece of rock and try to show how solid it is. Begin by using black and white paint on grey sugar paper. These materials will help you to show the variations between extreme light and extreme dark. You could also make other drawings, using soft pencils or pen and ink lines, or any materials that will make light and dark *tones*.

3 Work on a smaller scale in your sketchbook. Use a piece of typewriting paper and crush it gently in your hand. Make some pen and ink drawings. Imagine the up and down journey that a tiny insect would make in walking over the surfaces.

4 Try this idea using a sheet of newspaper. The *lines* of the columns will help you to see changes of directions.

Irregular forms

a piece of brown wrapping paper
sugar paper/construction paper
black and white paint
viewfinder

There are lots of ways of twisting and bending paper to make *form*. Pick up a small piece of brown wrapping paper and crush it up in your hands. This changes a two-dimensional rectangular shape into a three-dimensional form.

1 Put the crumpled paper on to a stool or chair. Use your viewfinder to look down on it through half-closed eyes. This will help you to see clearly how the light falls on the projecting pieces and leaves dark shadows in the crevices. These light and dark *tones* make the object appear solid. If you move the chair so that the light falls from a different direction, you will see the tones

Above left
Changing the two-dimensional shapes of a jigsaw puzzle into three-dimensional forms. Various tones of mauve and blue gouache on white card. (15)

64

Opposite
A pencil drawing of a piece of crumpled paper. The use of light and dark tones describes the form. (14)

Above
Sheets and blankets make an unusual 'landscape' to be explored in this large pen and ink drawing. (17)

Assemblage

about ten matchboxes
small three-dimensional oddments/remnants
p.v.a. glue
piece of wood or hardboard for the base

When we put objects together in a room, we are arranging all kinds of three-dimensional forms. Books fill the spaces on shelves, potted plants sit on tables, armchairs are ready to be occupied by people.

Make a collection of small, three-dimensional objects to arrange together. A good place to look is a drawer in a workshop or garage. See if you can find offcuts of wood and metal, nuts, bolts, screws, bits of electrical equipment and other oddments. All these things have interesting shapes and textures to work with.

1 Try some of these pieces together on a firm base of wood or hardboard. Build them up to make a construction that you can enjoy looking at from different angles.
2 Ask a friend to rearrange the pieces in another way and notice how the composition changes. Go on moving the pieces about until you are satisfied. Stick everything together with p.v.a. glue.
3 Try a similar method with the inside trays of matchboxes. Collect about ten boxes and try out a variety of arrangements. Walk round and look at other views of the construction.
4 When you have found the arrangement that pleases you, mark the positions and stick the boxes together with p.v.a. Using match box trays, you have found a method of designing a simple structure with recessions and projections. Look at buildings and you will see that architects have similar problems on a larger scale.

Above right
Assemblage. Oddments glued to a base and sprayed with matt white paint. (14)

Opposite
Louise Nevelson: Black Wall.
1959, painted wood, 112 × 85$\frac{1}{4}$ × 25$\frac{1}{2}$in, Tate Gallery, London. Scraps of furniture have been assembled together in boxes so that each contains a separate world of shapes which combine to make a whole new structure. Notice how each section contributes its own individual pattern of receding and projecting forms.

Carving

7lb bag of dental plaster
small cardboard box
plastic mixing bowl
sharp knife
glass paper

You may have already tried carving pieces of wood. Any shop stocking equipment for making models is likely to have solid 2 x 2in balsa wood which is soft and easy to carve, though any material can be used that is soft enough to be cut with a sharp knife. Walking in some parts of the country you may come across pieces of chalk that will also make good carving material. Alternatives are blocks of salt, soap and plaster. Builders plaster can be used but dental plaster, available from a chemist, is more refined and easier to carve.

1 Find a cardboard box about the size you want to use for your carving. Reinforce the sides by tying a piece of string round them.

2 Half fill a plastic bowl with cold water. Sprinkle hand-
fuls of plaster into the water until the powder is heaped
up *above* the water level. *Do not stir.* Mix the water and
powder together with your hands until you begin to
feel the mixture thickening.
3 Pour the thickening mixture of plaster into the box and
leave it to set overnight.
4 Remove the cardboard box and use glasspaper (fine
sand paper) to smooth the surfaces of the plaster.
5 With a sharp knife take out rectangular shapes which
stay parallel with the original block.
6 Turn the block round. Notice how the whole structure
is affected by each piece that you remove. Aim to keep
all the shapes simple. Look at the pattern of light and
dark tones made by the light falling on vertical and
horizontal surfaces.
7 When you are satisfied with the final form use glasspaper to trim the surfaces that need refining.

Construction

assorted strips of balsa wood
balsa cement or p.v.a. glue
a sharp 'Stanley' knife
wooden base about 4 x 4in

We have thought about how an architect builds solid
forms up into space. See what you can do on a small scale.

1 Use strips of balsa wood to build up a simple construction made of verticals and horizontals.
2 Stick the main verticals to the base with balsa cement
or p.v.a. glue. Add some horizontal pieces to strengthen
the structure. Keep all the pieces at right angles to each
other. Look at the *shapes* made by the spaces.
3 Try building another structure exactly the same.
Experiment by painting each in such a way that they
no longer resemble each other. You could use different
moods of colour or different arrangements of pattern.
In this way you will see how both *colour* and *pattern*
can appear to change *form*.
4 Make a drawing of your construction using *tone* to
emphasize its three-dimensional quality.

Opposite A painting based on a construction made of card. (16)

Top
Carving from a solid block of balsa wood. The recessed and
projecting shapes produce a pattern of tones. Height 6in. (15)

Above
Construction made from thin pieces of balsa wood. Notice how the
structure is enriched by the texture lines of the wood and the
dark shapes made by the areas in shadow. Height 4in. (16)

Above
'Sunflowers' by Vincent Van Gogh.
This famous painting was looked at carefully and analysed by a small group of children. They tried to memorise the different shapes of the individual flowers, the spaces between them, and the way in which the artist has arranged them so as to fill completely the rectangular shape of the canvas. Afterwards they each painted their own version, using their own colour schemes and patterns without referring back to the original picture. See page 152. Powder paint on sugar paper. 15 × 22in. (11)
('Sunflowers' picture reproduced by courtesy of the Trustees, The National Gallery, London.)

Top Left
A collection of discarded wrapping papers and scraps of wall paper was cut up and fitted together to build an imaginary city of colour and pattern. Selecting colours that create a particular 'mood' is just as important in collage as in painting. 19 × 24in. (16)

Left
A hockey match made out of pages taken from colour magazines, old postage stamps and a sheet of music. The tilting shapes and use of light and dark 'counterchange' suggest the movement of the players. See page 48. 10½ × 15in. (14)

2 Using the language

Starting points

The remarks I am about to make are intended to give you courage, for they will show how simple the matter really is. I ask, however, that you do not slavishly follow the schemes that are shown but merely take them as models for your own vivid creation. They are to serve merely to give you ideas.

Paul Klee

The first part of this book has shown you some ways of exploring the language of art. Now, using this language, you can go on to develop your own ideas. Of course, it is difficult to start from cold. All kinds of trivial things divert our attention and discourage us from beginning. The Irish playwright, Sean O'Casey, had an enormous notice pinned above his mantelpiece, saying 'Get on with the play': this dilemma of not knowing how to begin each time is common to most artists. In this second part of the book you will find suggestions for all kinds of starting points to help you over the problem.

You may have said, 'I have an idea in my head but I can't put it down on paper'. After a few attempts you have probably given up trying because that idea in your head is made of a different substance from the materials you are using. Forget about it: instead learn to *watch* what is happening on the paper as you work. Drawings, paintings and three-dimensional designs need to evolve, and each stage of their development is worth observing just as much as the finished product. Pause, look at what you are doing, and allow it to look back at you.

You are familiar with this way of working when you try to put down ideas for a story. Occasionally you may write everything down without making any alteration but more often you read what you have written and make some adjustments. Maybe you change words, alter their position, and rearrange sentences to make the right emphasis until the whole story sounds 'right'. There are similar problems in designing a picture.

When you reach a point where everything feels 'wrong', you sometimes need to push on further, as you do when you are writing. Look at your work in a mirror or turn it upside down and jolt your eyes into seeing afresh. This will help you to recognize the underlying structure of your design—the lines, shapes, colours, patterns, textures and forms. Be prepared to take risks, to overpaint and make changes. Through these decisions you will see your ideas growing as you work. That elusive 'idea in your head' will come alive on your paper.

Opposite
Taking a print from liquid oil paint dripped on to the surface of a tray of water.

Studies exploring structures seen at a railway station.

Doodles, blobs and drips

In such a daub one may certainly find a bizarre invention. I mean to say that he who is disposed to gaze attentively at this spot may discern therein some human heads, various animals, a battle, some rocks, the sea, clouds, groves and a thousand other things—it is like the tinkling of the bell which makes one hear what one imagines.

Leonardo da Vinci

Leonardo da Vinci was looking at marks that were made by throwing a sponge soaked in paint against a wall. If you have ever made up mental pictures from the light and dark shapes in the folds of a curtain, or from cracks and stains on an old wall, you have been thinking in a similar way.

Here are some simple ways of experimenting with materials to start your imagination working.

Doodles

1 With a ball-point or felt-tip pen, doodle on a piece of paper. Try to make your line continuous and allow it to travel in all directions. Stop after a few minutes and look at the result. Add to your drawing with any other materials that you feel like using.
2 Use the same method on a piece of paper that you have dampened with a wet rag.

Blobs

1 Fill the lid of an ink bottle with ink.
Pour a large drop of it on to a sheet of white paper.
Fold the paper in half; open it out again and look at the shape you have made.
2 Use the same method with several drops of different coloured inks. Turn the pieces of paper around until you begin to see something in the shapes and textures which will start you on a new idea.
Add any other materials that you want to use.

Drips

Try out any other methods that you can think of. Put a large sheet of paper on the floor and experiment with dripping paint from a tin, shaking it from a loaded brush and squeezing it from a sponge.

All these are different methods of applying paint to paper from the more conventional ones.

Creative doodling.

Although the effects are accidental, there is no reason why they should not be looked at seriously. Whatever you see can provide a starting point for your own ideas. Look at the work of the American painter, Jackson Pollock. In this way you will experience a dynamic use of paint that zips, twists, swirls and explodes across the surface of the canvas.

Senses and feelings

*sugar or cartridge paper/construction or drawing paper
powder paint or gouache
bristle and sable brush*

Some sensations only need to be put into words for us to be able to feel them in our imagination. See if you can hear and feel the whirr of a dentist's drill, smell a kipper frying, or taste a peppermint just by thinking about these things.

Do you think you could use paint to make equivalent feelings for one of these sensations? A brilliant, warm red certainly 'feels' different from a dull, murky green. A circle gives us a different feeling from a sharp pointed shape.

Here are some words to use in an experiment:

Noise: a dentist's drill, breaking glass, screams, drums, whistles.
Smell: kipper frying, burning rubber, ammonia, coffee, Camembert cheese.
Taste: peppermint, avocado pear, curry, peaches, chocolate.

Choose one of these words and see whether you can draw, paint or make a collage to suggest an equivalent. Select appropriate colours, shapes and textures without representing any objects or people.

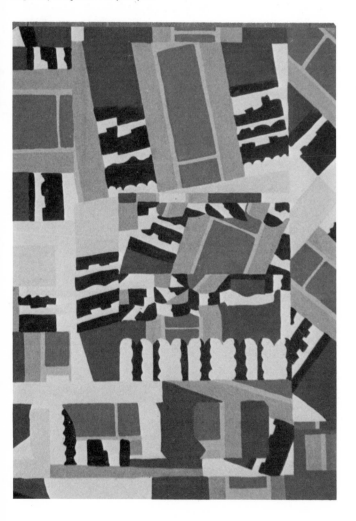

Left
Syncopation. Shapes and tones are used here to suggest a visual equivalent for jazz. (18)

Above
Enigma. A pencil drawing from an idea first constructed in three dimensions using thin white card. (17)

You may also like to find equivalents for other feelings. For instance: *anger, sadness, happiness, claustrophobia, confusion* and *speed.*

When you try these ideas, you will understand how artists became interested in making purely 'abstract' pictures—that is, pictures that are not concerned with representing scenes and objects drawn from life. A musician relies on sounds and rhythms to express his ideas and an artist can organize colours and shapes to build up a painting that can be enjoyed in a similar way to music.

Stretch a picture

cartridge paper/drawing paper
scissors
pencils, crayons or paints
magazines

Look through a magazine and choose a picture that interests you. It may be a landscape, a seascape, a group of buildings, or people, or whatever you like.

1 Cut an aperture 2 x 2in from a piece of paper. Move this about over the picture until it encloses a particularly intriguing detail. Cut this section out and stick it down on to a piece of clean cartridge paper. Put the remainder of the picture away.
2 Now study the section you have chosen and, using your own ideas, aim to extend the design outwards from all four sides.
3 Choose appropriate materials. Various grades of pencils could be used to extend a black and white photograph, while coloured crayons or paint could be used for a section in colour. You will need to observe carefully if you are going to match the *tones* and *textures* exactly. Without overpainting the cut section, try to integrate it into your design so that anybody looking at it will not realize that it is a separate piece.

All about you

card/poster board or strong paper
drawing materials
scissors
paint
cow gum/rubber cement

What is the shape of your nose? Which are your favourite colours. What do you like to eat? What do you enjoy doing? All these questions are about you. See if you can find some of the answers through drawings, photographs and bits and pieces that can be combined together to make a personal collage.

Here are some suggestions: take a print of your hand; collect some photographs of yourself; look in a mirror and draw a close-up of your mouth, eyes, etc; turn out one of your pockets and select any bits and pieces to use; collect a piece of textured surface that you enjoy touching; paint or collect samples of your favourite colours; hunt for words or phrases that you like and cut them out; collect pictures of something that you enjoy doing.

1 Take some ideas from these suggestions and add more of your own. When you have made a collection spread everything out on a large sheet of paper on the floor.
2 Stand up and look down on everything; this will help you to recognize the range of *shapes, colours* and *textures*.
3 Now move pieces about and take some away until you begin to see that your design is developing a feeling of *unity*. Walk round and look at it from all sides.
4 Mark the positions and stick everything down.
5 Pin the collage on the wall and think about adjusting parts by adding paint or other materials. Experiment: have the courage to try out any changes that occur to you until you feel that all the various pieces combine together to make a satisfying design.

Sea and rocks. The square photograph from which this painting began has been outlined here. (13)

to our own size. Knives and forks are made to fit a hand, a chair is the right size to sit on. But in a dream anything can happen. Familiar objects may be put into unfamiliar contexts or seen from strange viewpoints involving distorted perspective.

Make diagrams in your sketchbook to explore these and any other ideas that you may have. Remember to think not only about the idea in your head but to *watch* what is happening on the paper in front of you. Select materials that you think will best express your ideas, i.e. powder paint, gouache, coloured inks, crayons, collage, or perhaps a combination of these. Choose colours purposefully : aim to achieve a strong feeling of *unreality*. Look at Surrealist paintings, especially the work of Chagall, Magritte and Klee.

Left
Girl in space. The repetition of the figure and the sharp contrast of tone and texture emphasizes a feeling of fantasy. Collage of papers cut from colour magazines. (18)

Below
The dream. The use of a tunnel-like vanishing point and complex overlapping shapes heightens the dream-like quality in this painting. Gouache. (17)

Dreams and fantasies

any materials

We can illustrate ideas that seem to grow up in our minds and to come from nowhere at all. These are the pictures that we see when we sleep and dream. Waking up, the dream slides away and any attempt at describing it in words is usually a failure.

See if you can use this kind of elusive material as a starting point for a painting. I don't mean that you need to recall a dream you have had and paint that. Make up a new dream. Avoid the temptation to include a jungle of grotesque monsters; dreams are rarely like that. Instead try to experiment in a more positive way. Think about using changes of *scale*. Normally we see objects related

The Fire. Coloured chalks on brown sugar paper/construction paper. (15)

Illustrate stories

Now the rapidly spreading blaze had forced the partition into Mr Rumbold's premises, swept across his cellar, clambered in his garden by means of his well-tarred mushroom shed, and assailed the engine-house. It stayed not to consume but ran as a thing that seeks a quarry. Polly's shop and upper parts were already a furnace and black smoke was coming out of Rumbold's cellar gratings.
H. G. Wells

Words fill our minds with pictures. Shapes and colours grow to make us imagine people we have never met and places we have never seen.

Choose a story or a poem that you enjoy and read it again. While you are reading, concentrate on the pictures that come into your mind.

1 Try out some diagrams of these pictures in your sketchbook. Work within small rectangles so that you can see how the shapes are fitting together. Also make some notes about the colour mood of the story. Remember that you are not turning on a television set which gives you an immediate picture on the screen. The ideas on the screen in your mind need encouraging. Look at the lines that are growing on your paper; think of how you worked with doodles and blobs.

2 You may find that your memory is hazy about some detail that you want to include: perhaps the structure of a building, the shape and form of clouds or the way people move. Go out with your sketchbook and try to find the information that you need.

3 When you feel that your ideas are getting clearer, you can begin a larger picture. Choose the materials that would be appropriate. For a strong, bold picture like the fire described by H. G. Wells, you might use thick paint on a large piece of sugar paper. For a quieter, more delicate picture you could use thin washes of paint which can be drawn over with pen lines.

Remember that the words are only a starting point. No one will make the same translation from the story that you do. It is up to you to use your own feelings and ideas.

Sequences

cartridge paper/drawing paper
a variety of materials

There are some stories that could be better illustrated with a series of consecutive pictures rather than a single one. You know how a comic strip makes use of this method. This is not a new idea. It has been used many times before. A stained glass window is not only beautiful to look at, it also tells a story in a series of pictures. Many wall paintings, tapestries and manuscripts use a similar method; look carefully at some of these and you will see what I mean.

When we watch a film, we are unaware of the thousands of separate pictures which move across the screen to show us a sequence of events. Each day we make all kinds of consecutive movements without thinking about them. See if you can record some of your own movements.

Sequence of cleaning teeth. Gouache, pencil and pieces from colour magazines. (16)

Cleaning your teeth

1 Clean your teeth slowly and watch the sequence of movements in a mirror.
2 Make some notes about the different positions of your mouth, teeth, toothbrush and hand. Look for the simple shapes and only the minimum of detail.
3 Divide a piece of cartridge paper into about nine 3 x 3in compartments. Plan a series of simple line drawings to describe the sequence of movements made in cleaning your teeth.
4 If you want to add colour, choose your materials and decide on a simple colour scheme. You could use crayons, paints, inks, and other materials such as string, silver foil, and tissue paper.

The bank robber

Look at a television programme and imagine that your eyes are behind the camera. Watch the different angles that are used. Notice when the camera changes from a long shot to a close-up, or changes its point of view. You will see these things more clearly if you switch off the sound for a few minutes.

1 Imagine that you have been given the job of making a film about a bank robbery. Use any number of small compartments to work out a sequence of events. Aim to make the ideas flow from one compartment to the next.
Think about different positions for the camera.
2 Develop your ideas in more detail by asking a friend to play the part of the robber. Make drawings of him while he poses for you.
3 Use black and white gouache to make a range of grey tones and add textures with small pieces cut from a newspaper.

Use this method to describe other events that would be interesting to record in a sequence of drawings, for example, a game of tennis or a day in the life of an animal (facing page 97).

A personal collection

Most of us have an irresistible urge to collect pebbles from a beach. We feel that the ones worth having must be chosen by ourselves, for it is not at all the same if someone else collects them for us. At home, these pebbles, set out on a table, become something extra special—we look at them differently from the way in which we looked at the whole beach.

As mentioned in the 'Form' section, the sculptor Henry Moore has all his life collected inspiring bits and pieces—shells, pebbles, bones, pieces of rock—all of which can provide him with creative starting points. You yourself could begin to make a collection of objects which have a particular value to you because you enjoy looking at them.

Some of the best objects to start your ideas working are those where age and weathering has already begun the process of transformation. You may live near a piece of waste land, a scrap-metal yard, a demolition site or a junk shop: forage around and see what you can find. You will naturally select those objects which *your* eyes can transform into something new. It may be something like an old lock that takes on a special character when it is seen isolated from its context, or you may find smaller bits and pieces like seed pods or old tickets that look as though they would be interesting if they were combined together in a collage. At the time you may not know what you are going to do : put the collection in a bag, take them home and spread them out in your room. Leave them around and this will give your idea time to grow.

Apart from pieces of debris, you could make a collection of pieces from other kinds of discarded objects : broken clocks, radios and old car engines could be taken apart and the pieces transformed into completely new constructions. Experiment and try out anything that occurs to you. Be alert, keep your eyes open to recognize any bits and pieces that could build up your own personal collection.

Opposite
Waking up and going out to buy a newspaper. A sequence of pictures using carefully selected shapes cut from various tones of sugar paper.

Top right
A collage of pebbles and driftwood found at the seaside. (16)

Above
The base of a broken telephone painted in stripes of red, yellow and orange enamel. Coloured tops from detergent bottles have been fitted on a wire structure to replace the dial. (14)

Looking around you

I go for walks with no particular preconceived ideas. I have a very small notebook and I look right and left as I am walking, and suddenly, I see something that interests me and make a note of it. Then later I may come back and make a more complete note of it. These notes are extremely important as they are the basis of the final painting.

Graham Sutherland

Sometimes we find it difficult to think of a subject. For inspiration we need only to open our eyes and look around us to find that we are surrounded by a never-ending supply of visual ideas. To discover these ideas we need to draw. As soon as a drawing has begun we *know* that we are looking at things with new eyes. It is difficult to explain why this is so but it is certainly true. It is also true that it is no use waiting until we feel like drawing or until we see something that we *think* is inspiring. If we do this we will probably never begin at all.

Here are some clues that might provide you with interesting starting points: *earth, railways, docks, walls, fences, windows, doorways, movement, overlap.*

Of course this list of words means nothing much to you visually. You understand the meaning of the word 'earth' but this is not at all the same thing as examining a piece of ground closely, in the way that Graham Sutherland describes. I expect you could write a description of a railway station or a building site from memory, but what you would discover if you went to these places and made drawings would be quite different.

You can prove this by choosing a subject and going off by yourself with a sketchbook and allowing your eyes the chance to *observe*. It is no use going with friends because this will involve you in chatty conversations and you won't really *see* anything. Remember that an artist has to be a kind of sleuth, a private investigator, who

Landscape in Cornwall. Pen, brush and black ink. (18)

Above
Studies of men and tractors, with diagrams exploring ways of organizing a composition based on this theme.

Right
The final design built up with paper collage. Notice the careful selection of shapes, tones and textures (18)

never knows in advance what he is going to find. Aim to keep a section of your sketchbook for recording information about your subject over a period of time—perhaps at weekends or during holidays.

Perhaps you have had no experience of drawing outside and you are doubting if you will have enough courage. It certainly is difficult to stand still, take out a sketchbook and begin to draw, but the first few moments are the worst. Once you have begun you will forget your embarrassment and time passes quickly. I suggest that you gain confidence by drawing in the country, where you are unlikely to meet anyone else.

When you do begin to draw in a more public place, grit your teeth and pretend not to mind about people who stand idly around watching what you are trying to do. They will probably even make silly remarks which will make you feel like packing up and going away. Go on drawing in spite of these difficulties and if you can resist the temptation to answer your onlookers they will soon get bored and leave you in peace.

Of course you may want to use other means of research as well as drawing. You could take photographs, make rubbings to record textural surfaces, or collect relevant bits and pieces to add to your sketchbook.

On holiday

Last summer, I walked in a field near Avebury, where two rough monoliths stand up sixteen feet high, miraculously patterned with black and orange lichen, remnants of an avenue of stones which led to the great circle. A mile away a green pyramid casts a gigantic shadow. In the hedge, at hand, the white trumpet of a convolvulus turns from its spiral stem, following the sun. In my art, I would solve such an equation.

Paul Nash

The artist who wrote this was clearly excited by what he saw. His words describe his own very personal reaction. You could be in exactly the same place but what you would see, through your own eyes, would be quite different. Many people believe that artists look for conventional *artistic* subject matter. This may be a picturesque harbour with brightly painted boats, a famous beauty spot

Fishing in Connemara. Watercolour and black ink (14)

with breathtaking vistas, or the rose garden of a country cottage. Surely, they think, these subjects cannot fail to produce a beautiful painting.

In fact such places make us think of 'ready-made' pictures—they prevent us from really *seeing*. Instead we try to copy some idea that is in our minds about what we should produce—a kind of souvenir, a coloured picture postcard. It would be better to use a camera or to buy a postcard from the local shop.

On my first visit to Venice it seemed that all the paintings and photographs that I'd previously seen had suddenly come alive. I was actually there in that beautiful place. But when I settled down to draw, I found that it was an impossible task. My eyes were only able to see all the preconceived pictures that filled my mind.

You can see that the subject matter does not necessarily produce a good painting. Take your drawing equipment when you go on holiday but avoid those subjects listed in the guidebook. Find something less awesome that interests you personally. You need not necessarily aim to make a finished picture on the spot, but aim to collect information which would be of use to you in painting a picture at home. At first you will probably try to record too much detail, without searching for the broad structure of the main shapes and colours. The best way of finding out how to make notes on the spot is by seeing if you can work from them later at home. In this way you will discover how useful your information is. This is a real test. Being several hundred miles away from your holiday place, without the information that you really need, can be very frustrating. But this experience will help you to know how to improve your notes and what to look for next time you are out drawing.

Friends enjoy receiving a holiday message from you. Instead of buying picture postcards why not take a packet of plain cards with you and make your own individual drawings in coloured crayons or pencils.

Top
Harbour, South Wales. Page from a sketchbook. (17).

Above
Village church. Simple line drawings like this would make interesting holiday postcards to send home. (12)

Left
Scene from a swimming gala. Gouache. (13)

Drawing a house from memory. Coloured felt-tip pens. (11)

piece of paper, and this time go and look at the building and make another drawing outside.

It is interesting to put the two drawings together and compare them. In each of them you can see how you have been *thinking*. The first drawing shows what stays in your memory when you use your eyes in a casual way, and the second shows what your mind chooses to select when all the details are in front of you.

It is likely that both drawings showed the front view of your house. This is the obvious way to think about it but there are other ways. For instance, if in your imagination you remove one of the walls, you have a *section* through the house which reveals what is happening in several compartments at once. A *map* would include the house in the context of others in the same district. An estate agent would show a prospective buyer a *plan* to describe the shapes of the rooms.

All these views are to do with the same building and they all contribute to the identity of your house. There are many things to select from when we begin to draw. Our choice depends on the kind of information we want to give. You might like to try drawing a map, a plan and a section, as alternative ways of describing your house.

View through a doorway. Page from a sketchbook. (14)

Draw your house

sketchbook
cartridge paper/drawing paper
drawing materials
oil pastels or coloured crayons

Think about your house or the flats where you live and make a drawing from memory. Go on drawing until you have remembered as much as possible. Then take a new

This pencil drawing describes an intriguing jigsaw of shapes made by a potted plant seen against a view through a window. (18)

Each pane of glass in this window contains a different view. Chalks and paint on sugar paper/construction paper. (15)

View from a window

Windows are useful. They give us so many different views of our surroundings and we can sit and draw or paint, in comfort, on days when it is too cold or wet to be out. Choose a window with a view that you enjoy and think about the materials that you want to use. Here is a good opportunity to try out a new method of working. Choose whichever of these you have not yet tried.

1 *Watercolour*: use your paint-box and a medium-size sable brush and, *without any preliminary drawing*, paint the main shapes so that the white paper underneath shows through and makes the colours look transparent. You may prefer to use tubes of watercolour paint rather than a paint box. Gouache could also be used but this will give you an opaque instead of a transparent quality.

2 *Coloured inks*: use thinly in a similar way to watercolour and watch the way that new colours appear through overlapping shapes. Try drawing over this with a pen.

3 *Black and white wax*: cover a piece of card all over with white wax crayon and then cover this completely with a layer of black wax crayon. Use a pointed tool, like a thin nail or a safety pin and draw into the surface to reveal the white underneath.

Have you ever thought of designing your own personal book-plate? A view through your window would be a good basis for one.

Seeing with a camera

I'm interested in revealing the subject in a new way, to intensify it. A photograph is able to capture a moment people can't always see with their eyes.

Harry Callahan, *Time-Life* Photographer

The artist Paul Nash, who was quoted earlier, not only drew and painted landscapes, but he also used a camera to record effects of sun and shadow and close-up textural qualities. His photographs are not just casual snapshots. He succeeds in communicating the pleasure and excitement that he must have felt when he looked at the trees, rocks and other natural forms.

Anyone can use a camera but, as in drawing, our eyes must learn to see *selectively*. Only a slight movement of the camera in any direction will completely change the balance of *shapes* and *tones* that appear in the photograph. Just looking through the viewfinder helps our eyes to recognize the visual qualities of the subject.

Any simple inexpensive camera will be quite adequate for your first attempts. Later, when you become interested in a more experimental approach to photography, it will be worth buying a camera with a range of apertures and shutter speeds. An expensive but versatile camera is called a 'single lens reflex' and with this it is possible to record intriguing close-up detail.

The important thing about any camera is that it can make us more alert to the world around us and by looking with real curiosity we can find endless ways of enriching our visual vocabulary. Fleeting movements of people, animals and birds are often too quick for our eyes to register but they can be captured by the camera and held in a frozen moment of time for us to study at leisure. This applies to all kinds of other elusive qualities like reflections in windows, mirrors and pools of water.

You will find that all kinds of new visual ideas occur to you when you go out with a camera. You could begin to investigate a familiar place and see what you can

Opposite
A journey. Two friends worked out this sequence together, one walking and the other recording with a camera. Notice the range of viewpoints from long shots to close-up details. (18)

Using a camera to collect information about the structure of a deckchair. (15)

discover. The place might be your own garden or a small area of your school surroundings, or perhaps a local building site. Walk about and use the viewfinder of the camera to help your eyes to be *selective*. Avoid a series of vague, general views, and get in close to your subject. Aim to use your camera to search for hidden clues—to record details and facts that you have never noticed before.

Other starting points would be recording information about a wide variety of textural surfaces or searching for examples of pattern structures (see pages 50 and 58). You could think about combining photographs, drawings and writing together to make your own 'visual diary'.

Discovering familiar objects

'What a curious feeling!', said Alice, 'I must be shutting up like a telescope.'

And so it was indeed: she was now only ten inches high, and her face brightened up at the thought that she was now the right size for going through the little door into that lovely garden.

Lewis Carroll

After drinking from a magic bottle, Alice has shrunk into being a tiny creature and was astonished by the size of the things around her. If we could shrink, we too might be able to surprise ourselves into seeing quite ordinary objects in a fresh way. We get so used to the things which surround us that we think we know what they look like already. Therefore we sometimes draw in a lazy way and make up from our memory what we think we *should* see. Naturally this leads to dull, superficial drawing and to go on in this way would mean that we make no progress.

A drawing that is made with a really enquiring eye is likely to surprise us. It will certainly show us more than the 'reality' of a casual glance. In this section we are going to look very closely at some ordinary things and see what we can discover about them.

Enlargements

large sheet of sugar or cartridge paper/construction or
*   drawing paper*
assorted materials
any small object, e.g. press-stud, walnut, electric plug,
*   cake, wrapped sweet, toy, match-box, cotton reel, pin.*

We are going to take a small object and change the scale completely. Advertisements on giant hoardings do this all the time. We are used to seeing a bottle 20ft high, enlarged from a few inches. We hardly notice the change in scale; it seems quite normal.

You can experiment to find out how it feels to 'blow-up' a tiny object. Choose one from the list above, or find one of your own choice.

1 Pick the object up, turn it round in your fingers and examine it closely. Think about the materials that would be suitable to express the particular character of the object. For instance, a collage of brightly coloured papers could be used for a fat, shiny toffee. Matt, clear gouache might be appropriate for a match-box. A mixture of chalks, paints and paper could be used to build up the image of a cake.

2 Find a really large piece of paper, at least 20 x 25in and enlarge the small object until it fills the whole page. You will find it helpful to work on the floor. In this way you can stand up and look down, or stand up on a chair so that you get a kind of aerial view. This will help you to see where you need to make alterations. Finally, pin up your picture and walk back from it. Decide if there is anything more that you need to add.

Mechanisms

By looking closely at mechanisms we can see how the parts have been assembled together to make a functional structure. Take the back off a watch, and you will see a tiny world of carefully balanced shapes. A clock will show you similar shapes on a larger scale.

Look for an interesting piece of mechanism that you can study closely. Anything discarded that could be taken apart, like a broken clock, radio, or television set, would be ideal.

Make drawings in your notebook which will help you to understand more about the structures. If possible take the object to pieces and make diagrams to explain how it could be re-assembled.

Think about how you could use these drawings as the basis for a painting.

Left
The inside of a clock reveals an intriguing assemblage of forms.
Pencil and gouache on cartridge paper. (15)

Above
These cotton reels have been enlarged to fill the paper completely.
Imagine how you might feel if you were small enough to walk
around this strange 'landscape'. Black, white and brown chalks on
grey sugar paper. (17)

Viewpoints

sketchbook or sugar paper/construction paper
any household object, e.g. cup, kettle, plug, torch, lamp,
* camera, telephone*
assorted materials

Now I would like you to think about how an object can be
looked at from a number of viewpoints.

1 Choose any three-dimensional object that is easy to
handle. Try to imagine that you have never seen this
object before: it has fallen from outer space and your
job is to make a series of drawings to collect information
about it. For instance, if you have chosen a cup, turn it
round in your hands and study it from all possible viewpoints. Look at it sideways in profile, and a three-
quarter view; look down into it, and hold it above your
eye level and look up at it. Each of these views contributes to the total *identity* of the cup and provides us
with information about its character.

2 Make drawings to record this information. Choose two
other objects and investigate them in a similar way.

3 Pin up your drawings and think about how you could
combine the various viewpoints in one design. Make
diagrams to explore ideas about *overlap, transparency
contrast* and *scale.* Perhaps you have never thought
about using several viewpoints in one picture but there
is really no reason why this should not be done. It was
the basis of the Cubist ideas explored by Picasso,
Braque and Gris (see page 34).

4 Enlarge your ideas on to sugar paper using charcoal
which makes an easily adjusted flexible line, or other
materials that you think are appropriate. Aim to work out
a well-balanced relationship of shapes within the
rectangle. When you feel you have achieved this,
decide on the materials to use for developing the design
in colour. Work out your own approach: there is no
ready-made answer.

Several viewpoints have been combined together to make this
design. The tablecloth and colander are seen from above, the
percolator and bottle from a side view and the box is seen from
below. New shapes have been made by showing an 'X-ray'
through the objects revealing the lines of the table underneath.
Powder paint on sugar paper/construction paper. (16)

One object seen from six different viewpoints. Each drawing
contributes to the total identity of the boot. Pen and ink on
cartridge paper. (14)

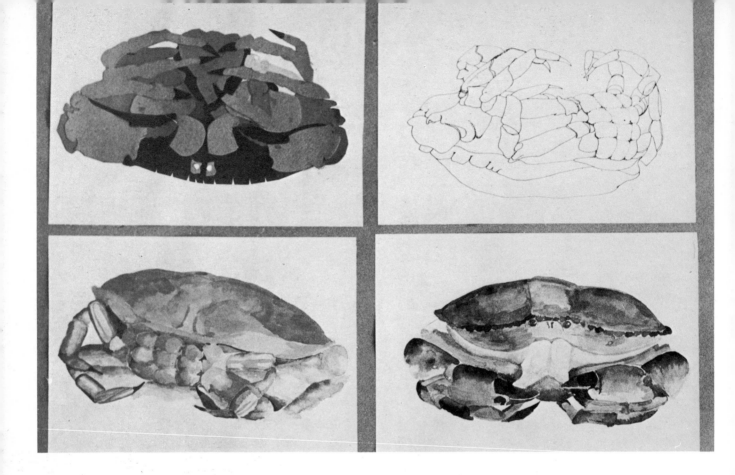

Studies of a crab from different viewpoints. Collage, pen and ink, and watercolour. (15)

Natural forms

sketchbook or cartridge paper/drawing paper
viewfinder
pencils

Nature is a marvellous source of inspiration for the artist. Plants, fruit, vegetables, shells, all natural forms can provide us with a wealth of information about colour, pattern, texture and shape. This is only superficially revealed by a casual glance; to discover more we need to search with an inquiring eye.

Suppose you start by observing plants. You may feel that these are so familiar that you know how to draw them before you begin. Because of this familiarity you need to look with a special alertness so as to avoid making up what you *think* you can see.

1 Select appropriate materials for your drawing. If you choose a pencil, you will do better without a rubber. You are more likely to make a real effort to look, for when you know that you can rub out every line, your effort weakens. Adjustment lines are your natural lines of thinking and nothing to be ashamed of.
2 Choose a plant and study it closely. Try to understand how the structure *works*. Look for the main lines of growth springing from the central stem. These make up the paths for the sap to travel upwards and into the

leaf veins. Although all the leaves on one plant have a similarity, it is important to notice that none of them are identical. Each has its own individual shape and position in relation to the other leaves.

In your drawing aim to search for these *particular* qualities and avoid making up vague generalisations. As in getting to know our friends we gain pleasure from encountering them as special individuals, so in drawing we can find most enjoyment in discovering the particular structure that makes each natural form unique.

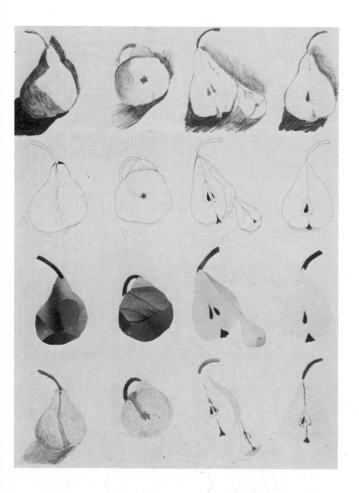

Left
Studies of a pear. Charcoal, collage and watercolour. (16)

Above
Study of ivy. Coloured crayons. (15)

Distortions

sketchbook or cartridge paper/drawing paper
various grades of pencil

The artist tries to look more intently than most people, so it is not surprising if he makes discoveries which can startle us. Have you been tempted to say, 'But surely that can't be right?', when you have seen a drawing which appears to distort an object?

Find an object made of shiny metal, like a steel saucepan or an electric kettle. Hold it up and look at your familiar room reflected in the surface. Strange things have happened. Certainly your face is changed and also the shapes of the objects in the room. They appear 'distorted'. This is another way of seeing things.

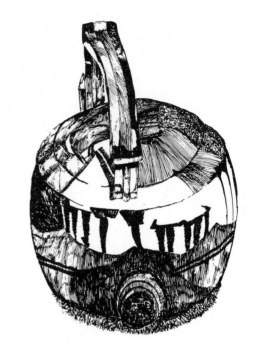

1 Make a careful pencil study of the *shapes* and *tones* that you can see in the surface of the kettle. Avoid a dull 'grey' drawing. A pencil can make a wide range of *tones* from light to dark. You might include the kettle in your drawing or you could just concentrate on one part of the reflection.

Mirrors also help us to see other aspects of 'reality'. Try this experiment.

2 Half fill a glass with water and stand it in front of a bottle. One containing oil or vinegar would be best but any bottle will do. Prop a small mirror up in a slightly slanting position behind the objects. Look carefully at the objects and their reflections. If you have another mirror, put it underneath the bottle and glass and see what a difference this makes. Use any materials you like to make drawings of the group from several different positions.

You may be able to think of other situations in which ordinary things appear quite different from how we imagine them to be. Think of how you might use some of these drawings as a starting point for a painting.

Opposite
Reflections on the surface of an electric kettle, and self-portrait seen in the concave, shiny surface of a spoon. Both pen and ink. (14)

Above
An intriguing jigsaw of coloured shapes made by the complex reflections of shiny tins and glass objects standing on a mirror. Gouache on white paper. (15)

Drawing portraits

We begin to make portraits when we first start to draw. These portraits describe how young children see their parents and friends. As we grow older we see quite differently and our drawings change. Portraits are not only a comment on the way that we see people but also on how we feel about them.

It is interesting to try this experiment. Make a drawing from memory of someone that you know well. Then ask them to sit still for you while you make a drawing from life. In your first drawing your memory will have helped you to select the details that you find interesting about that person. Your second drawing will be the result of more careful observation. Each drawing describes the person in a different way.

You may be dismayed by your inability to make a photographic 'likeness'. This kind of 'likeness' is the job of the camera. When you draw you are making a likeness of a different kind. The real face is translated into charcoal or pencil or whichever material is used. The result will be a description of what you have noticed and found interesting.

Here are some suggestions to start you off. You will see that making portraits is not limited to drawing people.

The 'face' of a car

A family car usually develops a particular character and often has a name to go with its personality. There are many ways in which you could make a portrait of a car but begin by studying its 'face'. You can get an interesting view if you sit on the ground and look straight at the front of the car. Make notes to find out about the structure of the parts and how they join together. Look at how the headlamps fit into the body to make eyes with pupils that light up at night. Include other things that make up the 'face'; the front bumper 'mouth' and number plate, radiator grille, and wing mirror 'ears'. Look for the distinc-

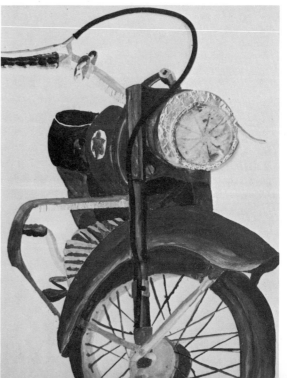

tive shapes that give the car its character.

When you have enough notes, use them to make your portrait in paint, crayon or collage.

Try a portrait of another piece of machinery, e.g. tractor, motor-bike, train, aeroplane.

Portrait of an animal

You probably know only too well how animals have an uncanny way of waking up and changing their positions just as you start drawing. Be prepared for this and use your sketchbook to make several drawings without worrying about completing each one. By persevering you will be able to go back to an unfinished drawing and add to it when the animal returns to his original position.

In drawing animals you will be surprised by the amount of information there is for you to discover. For instance, most of us have seen cats and dogs many times but it is really hard to remember all the details. When you think that you have done enough research, you can begin to plan your painting. A good way of working is to take the pages from your sketchbook and pin them together on a board propped up in front of you for reference.

I suggest that you begin by using charcoal to enlarge one of your studies on to a sheet of sugar paper. A rag will dust out the lines that need adjusting: the advantage of this method is that these lines remain like a ghostly image to remind you of your first drawing. If you rub them out altogether you are likely to repeat the same errors again. While you are drawing watch the new shapes that are being made between the animal and the edges of the paper. This is the area often referred to as the 'background'. I would like you to forget this word because it is particularly misleading: it suggests that this part of the picture is separate and rather unimportant. This is certainly untrue. As in a jigsaw, each shape affects the next shape, and to complete the puzzle *all* the shapes and colours must fit together.

You could continue the portrait using chalks or oil

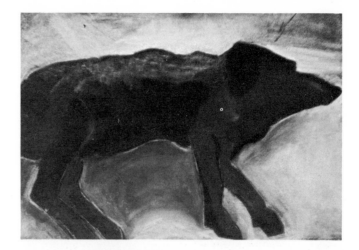

Top
'Buster' asleep. White chalk on black paper. (15)

Above
Portrait of a shrimp. Powder paint on sugar/construction paper. (12)

Page 96 above
Portrait of father, drawn from memory. Pencil and coloured chalks on sugar/construction paper. (11)

Page 96 below
Portrait of a motor cycle. Gouache, foil and black cord. (14)

Opposite
Six episodes in a cat's day. Powder paint and collage pieces cut from colour magazines. (17)

Facing page 96
Playing card portraits using counterchange patterns. (12)

pastels but, if you prefer to paint, then try using a thick consistency of powder paint or gouache applied with a bristle brush or a palette knife. Alternatively you could use thin, transparent watercolour or coloured inks on white paper. It is up to you to select appropriate materials for the animal that you choose to study.

Friends and family

Family and friends provide you with endless opportunities for drawing. Like cats, they are also likely to move and change position just as you begin. Persevere and try to get into the habit of making quick line drawings.

One way to paint a portrait is to show the person in their own surroundings doing something that interests them. Your brother may enjoy messing about with car engines. Draw him working in the garage rather than sitting in an armchair. Some people spend hours reading, watching television, or playing games of cards and chess. You can make a series of drawings of them to help you to build up a painting.

The person you are drawing is likely to say, 'Goodness, I didn't think I looked like that!' Don't be put off by this. We each have an idea of how we look and the closest we get to this is a flattering photograph which pleases us. The artist's mind does not work like a camera. He is able to organize his thoughts and feelings and the result is a different kind of 'likeness' from a photograph.

You may be able to encourage your friends and other members of your family to draw each other. Each one will see through their own eyes and all the portraits will be interesting and different.

Use your notebook for drawing people in cafes, on trains, in the park and on the beach. If you can't draw them when you see them, try to remember their positions and draw them later from memory.

Working from photographs

There are many different sources of information that make up our images of pop-singers, film-stars, comedians, sportsmen and other famous people. We may have actually seen them but it is more likely that we know them only through a mixture of magazine pictures, photographs,

Above
Grandfather, asleep. (16)

Above right
Drawing of mother. (17)

Below
Brother lying on the sofa. Acrylic paint and textured papers. (18)

Above
Friends talking. Pencil drawing in which sensitive use is made of a full range of tones from light to dark. (14)

Right
Alexander Solzhenitsyn. Drawing based on information taken from photographs. Coloured chalks. (16)

Your first impulse may be to make a tracing from one of the photographs in the hope that you will achieve some kind of 'likeness'. If you do this you will find that your drawing looks strangely artificial: you are copying in a mechanical way without understanding. For instance, photographs of galloping horses reveal that their legs leave the ground in a different way from the way that artists have always represented them in paintings. When this discovery was made and horses began to be painted as the eye of the camera sees them, everyone complained that the paintings looked wrong. As you know, the artist needs to observe and then to translate his own feelings and experience into a picture; this is what you must do whether you are looking at real life or at photographs. Certainly you need courage to pursue your own line of enquiry. People may admire your efforts if the finished work looks like the original photograph but apart from technical cleverness you yourself will have learnt very little.

Study the information which the photographs provide and aim to use this to build up a portrait. Select a characteristic position and an appropriate environment and choose materials and colours that you think will sum up that particular person.

posters, films and television. All these images blend in our minds to make a composite portrait.

You probably already have a collection of photographs of a famous person that you admire. Look at them closely and think about how you would make your own portrait of that person. Unlike studying your family and friends you will have to rely entirely on the information given by the photographs. As soon as you start to draw, you will find that some areas may show details clearly while others are blurred and confusing. On the other hand, because the person is frozen in a certain position this approach may seem easier than drawing from life. It is certainly a help to observe complicated actions in this way but the disadvantage is that however much you may need it you cannot get further information by moving closer or changing your position.

Self-portraits

sketchbook
cartridge or sugar paper/drawing or construction paper
any materials
mirror

You can settle down with a mirror and draw yourself at any time. Try out a series of portraits each using a different material—for instance, charcoal, pen and ink, crayons paint and collage. This will help you to understand the individual qualities of the materials and how they can be used, each in their own way, to build up the three-dimensional form of the face.

It is a good idea to work *outwards* from the centre of your face. If you start at the edges and work inwards, you are likely to find that you haven't left enough room for your nose. Look for important structural details—the distance and shape of the spaces between the corners of your nostrils, the corners of your eyes and the corners of your mouth. Relate these points to the positions of your eyebrows and ears. Notice that eyes are often about midway between the top of your head and the bottom of your chin. Look at the shapes made by your hair.

When you are drawing yourself, you have the opportunity to study a range of expressions. Make drawings to compare the differences between a smiling face and an angry one. Move the mirror into another position so that the light falls on to your face in a different way: try on hats and scarves. Think of any other ways of changing your face.

Rembrandt made self-portraits throughout his life, so did many other artists. Look out for examples of these in your local art gallery or in books.

If you feel like embarking on a really ambitious study, make a full length, life-size portrait of yourself. You will need to stick sheets of paper together and find a long wardrobe mirror.

Above
Self-portrait. Black and white gouache. (18)

Above right
Self portrait. Two bathroom mirrors provided the opportunity for this series of unusual self-portraits. (15)

Drawing from life

I am very busy painting those heads. I paint in the day-time and draw in the evening. In this way I have painted at least some thirty already and drawn as many. With this result, that I see a chance of doing it better ere long, I hope.

Van Gogh

Those of you who enjoy drawing people will be interested in studying the human figure more intently. To do this you need time, concentration and a willing model.

It is easy to believe that there is some special 'knack' required for drawing people. Perhaps this is because we have seen the work of cartoonists who appear to suggest a 'likeness' with a few deft strokes which exaggerate an easily recognizable characteristic of a particular person. The kind of likeness that we are concerned with will be the result of careful *observation*. Certainly, drawing the human figure involves us in all kinds of difficult choices and decisions, but there is no need to put it in a special category apart from other drawing.

If you can persuade a friend to sit quietly reading a book or sleeping, you will have the opportunity to study him intently. Here are a few suggestions to help you.

1 Sit quietly yourself and try to select an approach to your drawing. Just as in drawing a tree (page 20) you need a positive attitude. Look through a viewfinder. Walk round the room and look at your friend from other positions.
2 Decide which point of the figure is *nearest* to you and which is *furthest* away. Can you feel that the person is occupying *space* in the room and is therefore *solid* and three-dimensional? We have already seen how solid objects are affected by light: some surfaces face the main source of light while others recede from it (page 62–3). Half close your eyes and look at these light and dark *tonal contrasts*, and imagine yourself journeying like a tiny insect over this human landscape, up hills, down slopes and across uneven ground.
3 Think about which materials you should use. This will depend on whether you want to work in *line*, in *monochrome* or in *colour*. Imagine how you will place the figure on your paper so that it makes a well-balanced shape within the rectangle.

Top
Girl lying on a striped rug. Chalks on sugar/construction paper. (15)
Above
Girl walking. Have you tried drawing people in movement? You have to work at speed and aim to select only the most important shapes. Drawing directly with a large brush and liquid paint helps to eliminate unnecessary details. (15)

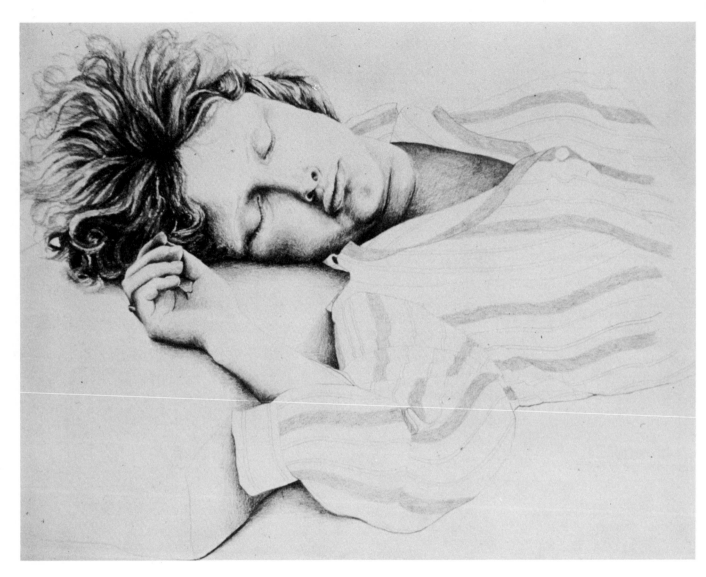

4 Begin by drawing the whole figure very lightly. You need to think about the underlying structure of the skeleton. This is our own structure. It is helpful to get into the same position yourself and feel what happens to your own body and limbs. The body is centred round the spine and all movements are related to this. Look for the direction in which the spine bends, the slope of the shoulders, the tilt of the hips and angle of the head.

It is no use observing smaller details until you have worked out the basic structure of these main shapes. This is really quite difficult as it requires persistence and keen observation. You will find that you are getting the shapes roughly in the right place and are eager to go on to the next stage. If you want to explore figure drawing you must be much more disciplined.

The intriguing thing is that in each drawing you yourself can discover a particular jigsaw of shapes that will never be exactly in those positions again. Ask your friend to move and change his position. As soon as he does you will see the shapes shift like pieces in a kaleidoscope. If you are fascinated by this you will certainly enjoy drawing people. Remember that you are observing those shapes as they are at that particular moment. In this way you will discover far more than if you look casually and more or less make up what you think your drawing *should* look like. A simple method of checking your accuracy is with a pencil held upright or horizontal with your arm fully extended. Close one eye and move the pencil to measure angles and distances between points. Imagine a vertical line extended down from the chin and check the exact points at which it would touch other parts of the figure and chair. Do the same thing using different starting points.

5 When you are satisfied with the main structure you can begin to explore in more detail. Look at the shape of the fingers as they hold a book, at the way in which a shirt collar wraps round a neck, or sleeves round a wrist. Choose from the *lines* and *tones* that you see those that you think will best explain the *form*.

I have given you a few suggestions for ways of working but there is no end to what you can discover. Whatever you do you will almost certainly be dissatisfied with the result because the more you concentrate and look intently, the more likely it is that your eyes will become sharper and more critical and you will want to try again and again.

Studying a figure from an unusual angle sharpens our awareness. This foreshortened view provides unexpected shapes and emphasizes the solid 'landscape-like' qualities of the figure. Powder paint on sugar/construction paper. (17)

Opposite
A sleeping figure gives the opportunity to investigate subtle details of form. Compare lines chosen to describe the texture of hair with those defining the form of the shirt. Notice how pencil tones have been used to show that some surfaces face the main source of light while others recede from it. (18)

103

Transformations

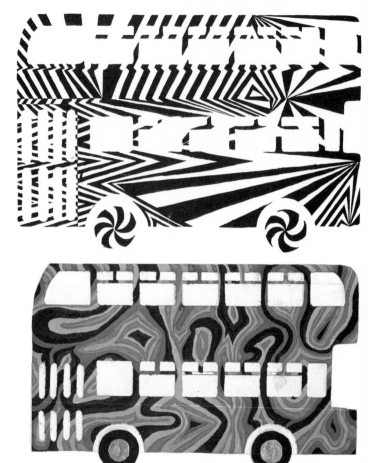

All art is transformation. It changes one substance into another. A landscape of earth, mountain and sky can become a landscape of pen, pencil and crayon. In the same way, sculptors can translate the human figure into stone, wood and metal.

Apart from this change of one substance into another, there are the gradual changes that take place in nature. We are aware of days changing into evening, and winter into spring, summer and autumn. A city at night looks quite different from the same place during the day time and a familiar summer landscape has a new character in winter.

Nature also changes us a little each day although too slowly for us to notice. We can change ourselves by wearing different clothes, using make-up or altering a hair style. An actor uses the same methods to transform himself into a new person on the stage.

Objects can be changed in a similar way. Some of the red London buses have recently been painted all over with giant advertisements and this has given them a completely new character. We can alter the whole look of a room by changing the colour of the walls and adding new shapes and patterns in furniture and fabrics.

Changing the appearance of objects is a fascinating thing to do. Try out some of the suggestions in this section and see if you can add more ideas of your own.

Camouflage

drawing and painting materials
tracing paper
cartridge paper/drawing paper

Now we are going to experiment with making four identical objects look different from each other. You could choose anything you like but here are some suggestions: a mug, coffee pot, car, armchair, even a

Above
Experimenting with pattern can change the familiar look of buses. Gouache. (16)

Opposite
Detail of 'stained glass' window (see page 112).

famous statue. Either make a line drawing of one of these or use a clear photograph.

1 Make a tracing from the drawing or photograph. Include only the most important lines. Add four lines to enclose the drawing in a close-fitting rectangle.
2 Trace this four times on to another sheet of paper so that the rectangles are touching, above each other or side by side.

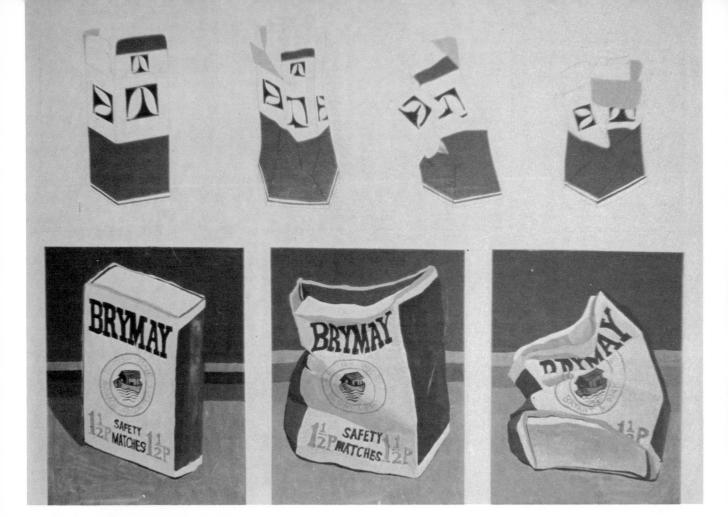

Above
Studies of new shapes observed during the action of crumpling
up a tea packet and an empty match-box. Pen, ink and gouache. (17)

Opposite
Still life. Powder paint on sugar/construction paper. (12)

3 Paint or crayon the first picture in any way that you
   choose, including the background.
4 Paint or crayon the other pictures so as to make them
   as different as possible from the first one and from each
   other.

Explore the possibilities in using pattern, texture, colour
and tone to change the appearance of objects and people.

Squashing and crumpling

paper and drawing materials

We often change the appearance of objects without
thinking about what we are doing. We squash or crumple
up bags and packets to make them smaller when we
throw them away. In doing this we make a series of new
shapes until finally the screwed-up shape is put in a
waste-bin. This happens every day in the kitchen and you
can easily make a collection of empty detergent packets,
paper bags, cereal and tea packets and other containers.

1 Experiment by squashing these objects in slow motion until you have decided which one would be most interesting to draw.
2 Make a series of drawings, either in your notebook or on a piece of cartridge paper, to show the changes in shape as the object is gradually squashed. Think about making good use of the shape of your paper and choose materials that you think would be appropriate.
3 You may use a packet with lettering on it. If you want to include this, use it purposefully to emphasize the changing *structure* of the form.

Assembly kits

HB pencil
white card/poster board
sketchbook
sable brush
gouache

You may be familiar with the kits which provide models in separate pieces to be assembled together. The picture on the front of the package reassures us that all the small plastic shapes inside will eventually become the machine that it represents. The component parts look very strange in isolation but they can indeed be magically transformed into the model itself.

A similar method is used in less ambitious models where a single sheet of card contains all the parts ready to be pushed out, or cut with scissors.

Try this for yourself. You will need a small model or toy, preferably one that does not take apart. A toy aeroplane or car would be suitable.

1 Look at it carefully and think how to change it into a flat assembly kit. Aim to select the basic pieces that would need to be fitted together to re-make the model in three dimensions. Make diagrams in your sketchbook.
2 Draw these pieces on to a single piece of white card. Try to arrange them compactly.
3 Add colour and necessary details.

Any man-made object can be taken apart in this way. Try inventing a paper pattern for an existing dress or diagrams for constructing a piece of furniture.

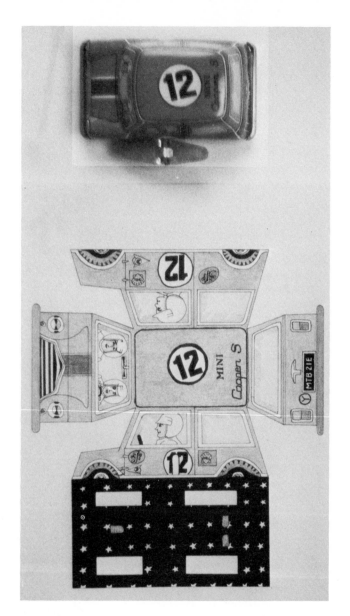

Above
A three-dimensional toy car can be changed into a two-dimensional assembly kit. Coloured pencils and ink. (16)

Opposite
Enlargement from a toy motor cyclist. Gouache and silver paint. (17)

Change of identity

drawing materials
sketchbook

Have you ever looked at objects and turned them over in your mind until they become something similar but different? A gnarled piece of driftwood may look like a fossilized dragon. A chunk of rock may suggest a human head.

See if you can work out some deliberate transformations of quite ordinary objects. Choose two that have some slight affinity and see if you can make a series of consecutive drawings to change one gradually into the other. Perhaps a telephone has the possibility of growing into kitchen scales, a horse-chestnut leaf into a glove or a tin-opener into a pair of glasses.

Try out some ideas in your sketchbook and see what you can do.

Optical illusions

black and white paper
scissors
cow gum/rubber cement

Doodling, especially with a ruler, a pair of compasses and a pad of graph paper, can produce all kinds of optical effects which appear to transform a flat piece of paper into three dimensions. You have probably already discovered this; if not, see what you can do with black ink and a white piece of paper.

Besides making optical effects of three dimensions it is also possible to produce a positive sensation of movement. This sensation, which we feel through our eyes, can give us feelings of visual jumpiness and discomfort. These feelings are strongest when we look at the contrast between black and white. A fabric made of black and white checks makes a far more powerful impact on our eyes than a similar pattern using two close tones.

Here are some experiments for you to try.

1 Cut up some black and white paper into a variety of small squares. Try out different arrangements on a white

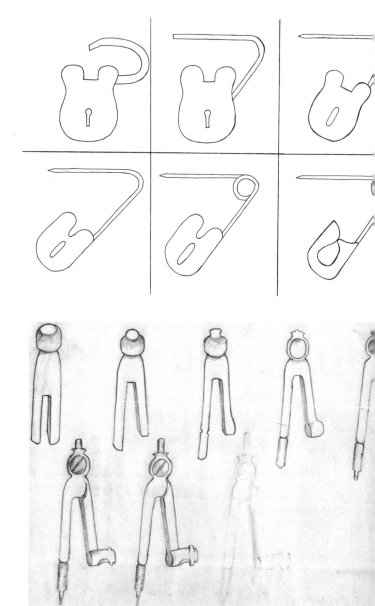

Top
In five moves a padlock can grow into a safety pin. (15)

Above
A clothes peg/pin dances itself into a pair of compasses. (15)

background, aiming to produce a really 'eye-jumping' effect. When you feel that you have succeeded, stick these pieces down.

2 With scissors cut several curving lines across a 6in square of black paper. Move these pieces about on a white background until you feel an energetic interaction between the black curves and the white shapes between the curves. Stick the pieces down. You could add black pen lines to see if this will accentuate the feeling of movement.

Try this idea using a rectangle and then a circle.

Look at the work of Bridget Riley and Victor Vasarely—two artists who have explored the visual excitement of optical phenomena based on precise mathematical calculations.

Above
Squares of black paper divided and rearranged so as to create a lively interaction with the new white shapes appearing in the background. (13)

Right
This three-dimensional model of a foot appears flattened against the background because both the plaster cast and the board have been overpainted with a confusing pattern. (16)

Working with friends

There are times when it is enjoyable to work with a group of friends or with other members of your family. This would be a good opportunity for making a large mural; each one of the participants designs a section and works on it simultaneously with the others. When you have a number of people working together it is surprising how quickly these large-scale designs can be made.

Murals can decorate a wall in or outside your house, or in your own room. They can also be temporary decorations put up for a birthday or Christmas party. Any number of people can help if you divide the space into small sections.

A flower mural

sheets of sugar paper/construction paper
4B pencils
powder paint or gouache
sable brushes
flowers

Here is a method for making a flower mural. You could use a similar method for other themes.
1 Collect some flowers to look at. Your own pressed flowers or magnified details from books of photographs would be helpful.
2 Measure the wall and decide on a good size of unit to divide it into, i.e. a 6 x 6in square or larger.
3 Cut up sugar paper to the size you have chosen and give a section to each person.
4 You are each aiming to fill the squares with a *pattern* of simple shapes based on a flower structure. Several details from different plants could be fitted together as the flower is not intended to be naturalistic but decorative. Imagine you are seeing it pressed flat between two pieces of glass.

Above
Young people worked together making a mural to transform this section of a peeling outside wall. Pebbles and glazed pottery shapes were sunk into squares of cement.

5 Draw the big shapes of the petals first and gradually work in towards the centre. Fill this with detail to make it really intriguing to look at closely.

6 Decide on a colour scheme so that the separate units link together. If you want a cool-looking wall, then each person must mix a variety of different blues, mauves, greens, greys and whites. For a warm, glowing decoration, you need variations on pinks, reds, oranges, yellows and browns.

7 Mix a background colour for everyone to use. If the flowers are light in tone, then the background should be dark.

8 When you have all completed enough squares, arrange them on a strong cardboard base and stick them down carefully so that all the edges join together. If the wall already has a 'pin-up' surface, then you could pin the squares directly on to this.

A 'stained-glass' window

sheets of sugar paper/construction paper
black powder paint or gouache
bristle brush
charcoal
sharp trimming knife and scissors
coloured tissue paper (*the more the better*)
cow gum/rubber cement

Another interesting method of transforming a room, only this time by altering the windows or glass panels, is by applying paper 'stained glass'.

This looks marvellous with the light coming through it at Christmas time and you will really enjoy making it. Go and look at a real stained-glass window or, if this is not possible, get a book of pictures from the library. Look carefully and notice these details :

a The design is drawn with a thick *line* made of lead.
b Complicated, natural shapes are changed into simplified, flat shapes.
c All the lines have to touch each other so that they can hold the *shapes* of coloured glass in position.
d Only a few colours are needed to make a rich design.

Above
Preliminary drawing for the 'stained glass' window, a detail of which appears opposite page 104. (12)

Opposite
Painting the design with strong black lines. Cutting round the edges of the lines with a sharp blade and removing the paper so as to leave empty spaces for the coloured tissue paper.

Facing page 113
Still life. Powder paint on sugar paper. (12)

Before you can work on a large scale, you must plan your ideas on a smaller piece of paper. Measure your chosen window and draw it to scale: 1in = 1ft.

1. Decide on a subject. This could be an illustration of the Christmas Story or a display of your town's activities or just a rich decorative pattern.
2. Draw your idea in simple, clear lines, remembering that *all* the lines must touch each other.
3. Use just a few colours to plan a colour scheme.
4. Draw clear lines across the design to divide it into enough sections for the number of people who are taking part. If necessary, each person could make more than one section.
5. Make a tracing of the design. Number the sections on both the design and the tracing. Cut the tracing up so that each person has a piece to work from.
6. Cut up sheets of sugar paper to the full size for each section. Number them in the same way.
7. Draw a 2in border round each one and fill it in with black paint. This makes a firm edge to hold the lines.
8. Using charcoal, enlarge each small section on to the sugar paper. Everyone must check that the lines of each enlargement link across with the others.
9. Go over the charcoal lines with black paint. Make them at least $\frac{1}{2}$in wide. They must be broad enough to support the tissue paper shapes in between.
10. Put the sugar paper flat on a piece of cardboard, and with a *sharp* blade cut away the unpainted areas.
11. Hold sheets of coloured tissue paper against a window and look at the colours. Try mixing the colours by layering several pieces together. The strong light from the window bleaches colour from a single sheet, so the more sheets you use the better.
12. Put the black framework over the colour you want, and mark round the edges with pencil.
13. Cut out $\frac{1}{4}$in away from the pencil line, and using a small amount of cow gum, stick the tissue into position. Add other layers of tissue paper behind this until you arrive at the colour you want. Test by holding against a window.
14. Go on filling in the other spaces. Be sure not to leave any gaps where the light can show through.
15. Finally, join all the sections together with gummed tape on the back. Fix to the window with sellotape.

Colour slides

empty slide frames
sellotape/Scotch tape
35mm projector

Here is another method of enlarging a picture. Tiny designs constructed in a colour slide can be enlarged with a 35mm projector.

Slide frames with glass fronts are preferable, but you can also remove the film from old reject slides and use these again. Your design can be made out of all kinds of tiny bits and pieces: scraps of coloured tissue paper and cellophane produce rich colour effects, and lines can be added with fine string or strands of cotton. Try pieces of leaf, especially a skeleton leaf, bits of twig and grass and pieces of fabric. If you are working with friends you can compare the effects achieved through using different combinations of materials.

1 Pieces can be put directly into a glass-fronted slide but an open slide needs a sticky surface to hold everything in place: this is made by stretching one or two strips of sellotape/Scotch tape across the open back.
2 Arrange a few pieces, put the slide into a projector and look at the result. If necessary add more pieces.
3 If you have a glass-fronted slide, drop in spots of coloured ink and watch the effect when you project it.

Enlarging in this way is similar to looking at slides under a microscope. Both methods are visually stimulating. They show us new and unexpected ways of using colour, shape and pattern.

Go on experimenting and try out other ideas.

Enlarging a picture

Here is an intriguing experiment to try with a group of friends. Choose a picture postcard that you would like to see enlarged as a mural.

1 Select a wall space and measure an area which is the same proportion as the original. Cut sugar or cartridge paper/construction or drawing paper to fill this size.
2 Rule lines across the paper and the postcard to divide them each into the same number of sections as the number of people taking part.
3 Write numbers on the back of the postcard to correspond with the same numbers on the back of the paper.
4 Cut the paper and postcard into their separate sections. Put the postcard pieces into a box so that each person can select a section at random.

The problem is to take your piece of the picture and enlarge it to fill your section of paper.

You must agree on the materials to use. It doesn't really matter which you choose but of course everyone must use the same. Powder paint or gouache, coloured crayon, or even coloured paper used as collage, would be possible.

5 Begin by assembling the sections of paper together and lightly drawing in the main lines of the picture *structure*. After this each person can work separately with an occasional test to see if the piece is relating to other pieces in the design. As the picture progresses some may prefer to work together rather than at single sections.
6 Finally fit all the pieces together and add any finishing touches that seem necessary.

The final result will be a translation based on the original. There is no need to worry about the differences which will occur. It is only to be expected that each person will add something of themselves to the reconstruction.

Opposite
Slide made from tiny overlapping pieces of coloured tissue, a
scrap of linen and a few grass seeds.

Right
Painting the enlargement of a postcard. Eight friends each took an
eighth part of the postcard and enlarged it from 2 × 1½in to
14 × 10½in. In this final stage of the work, the enlarged sections are
joined so that the total colour scheme can be assessed.

Above
Piccadilly Circus. To make this well balanced design, the original
was greatly simplified. People were left out and other confusing
details of traffic, advertisements and buildings were reduced to
simple shapes. Gouache on cartridge/drawing paper. 28 × 42in.
(16-18)

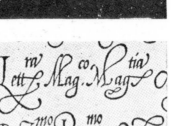

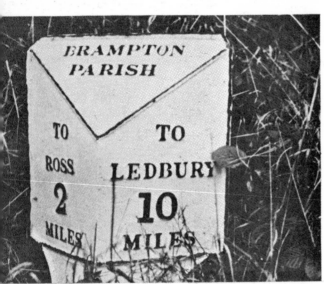

The alphabet

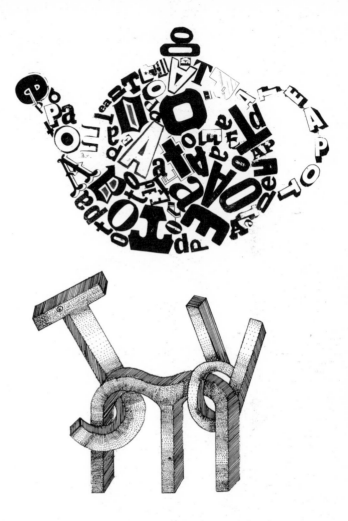

Our alphabet is made of shapes. Fat, round shapes, pointed tent shapes and simple squares and rectangles. We see these shapes all around us, every day. Letters larger than us look down from advertisement hoardings; others give us the information we need on road signs and buses. The page of this book is covered with smaller letter shapes which make up a code that we have learnt to read. By reading and understanding we may forget that each letter in our alphabet is an individual shape which contributes to a complex pattern.

We can understand this if we look at an alphabet that has no literal meaning for us. A Russian or Greek newspaper helps us to recognize at once the pattern of shapes that the letters make on the page. By turning this book upside-down, you will find it easier to see the kind of pattern made by letters in our own alphabet.

In this section we are going to begin by hunting for all kinds of different letters. You will find an almost endless variety of characters which you may have hardly looked at before.

Hunt for letters

scissors
cow gum/rubber cement
scrapbook
newspapers, magazines, packaging, leaflets

When you look at the shapes of letters, you will begin to see that they have different characteristics according to the different purposes for which the lettering is used. For example, the letter 'A' used on a road sign or a huge poster, has to be designed as a bold, clear shape easily read from a distance. Used on a book-jacket, the same letter may have a new shape to fit the kind of book it has to describe. Look along the bookshelf and notice the variety of letter shapes on the spines. Each group of

Opposite
Photographs of the alphabet in use. a. Roman letter. b. Italian neon sign. c. Euston Station. d. C16 writing book. e. German manuscript. f. Milestone. g. Lindisfarne Gospel. h. Boutique. i. Computer letters. j. French shop sign. k. Shop front. l. Italian terracotta.

Top
Six letter shapes make up the word 'teapot' and for each of these there is a wide range of variations. Here some have been cut out of newspapers and magazines and used to build up a collage. (14)

Above
Initials making an unusual three-dimensional monogram. (14)

117

letters has been specially designed and arranged to show the character of the individual book.

1 Hunt through old magazines, newspapers and discarded packaging and collect all the different examples you can find of letters and numerals. Notice the range of heights and widths. You will discover that the more elegant letters are drawn with both thick and thin lines and have little feet or serifs to complete them. Others are made of an equal thickness throughout. Can you think of reasons why these two kinds of letters were invented? Compare letter shapes on tins and packets and you will begin to see why certain shapes have been chosen.

2 Cut out the letters you have found and make an interesting collage. If you cut them carefully into squares and rectangles, you will be able to fit them together on a page. You could cover a school notebook or fill pages of your scrapbook.

3 Take a newspaper and cut out a wide range of different sized headings. Spread them out on a sheet of paper with some of the columns of type. To help your eyes to see the letters as *shapes*, turn the words upside down. Notice how the columns of type make a small, closely knit, grey pattern and the larger headings provide a strong contrast of black and white tones. The sentences could be kept whole or cut up into separate word or letter shapes. Experiment with using these shapes and tones to make a collage.

4 Apart from this vast range of letter shapes used by printers there are all the variations which we make for ourselves. Letters drawn by hand have the same individual and personal quality that is common to all drawing. Compare the shapes that you make in your writing with those made by your friends. As long as the letters remain legible, the differences are interesting.

   If you hunt around you will find other examples. Fishmongers use a brush and white paint to make a daily list of prices on their windows; railwaymen chalk up train delays; walls and fences provide a background for slogans. All these letter shapes have their own unique characteristics.

Above
Your name gives you your own personal set of letter shapes. Here the shapes of a name have been varied in size and thickness and rearranged with pattern and overlap. Felt-tip pens. (11)

Opposite
Can you find the name hidden in this pattern of letter shapes?

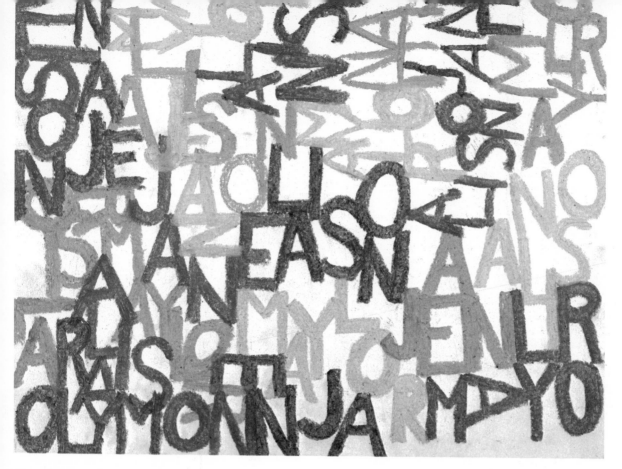

The shapes of your name

sketchbook or cartridge/drawing paper about 10 x 8in coloured felt-tips or crayons

By hunting for letters, you have met some of the different shapes that can be used to make up words. The shapes that you put together every day are the shapes of your own name. Try putting them together in a new way.

1 Use a coloured crayon or a felt-tip pen to draw the first letter of your name anywhere on the paper. Emphasize its character by making a bold shaped capital at least ½in thick.
2 Turn the paper round. Look at the shape from all sides. Add the second letter of your name so that it touches some part of the first letter and makes an interesting new shape.
3 Go on adding the other letters of your name. Make them have different characters, tall, short, fat and thin. Put them in any position on the page. They can be drawn sideways or upside down, but each one should touch another letter. Aim to fill the page completely.
4 Now you have a pattern of lines and shapes. Look at the new shapes made by the letters touching each other. Choose colours that work together to make up a particular mood, and colour the shapes with felt-tips or crayons. You are aiming to make an overall pattern where your name is now quite hidden.
5 Take your own initials and try ways of combining the shapes to make a monogram. Aim to lose the separateness of the letters.

119

Shiver, dwindle, bulge

Another way of using letters is to design them so that the shapes themselves *suggest* the meaning of the word. All advertising does this to some extent. The designers of posters, food packaging, record sleeves and book jackets, each need to select particular letter shapes which can relate to the subject. Thick black letters appropriate for advertising car tyres would be out of place on a perfume bottle: the cover of a book about roses must present a different image from a science-fiction thriller.

This use of shapes to suggest meaning can be taken much farther. Think about these words and see if you can invent letter shapes that actually *look* like their meaning: *fat, thin, tired, speed, fall, shatter, bounce, jump, jagged, spiky, spring, decorative, lazy, groan, smile.*

Make a poster

'Imagine', he said, 'that you have a small measuring glass. It holds, of course, just so much water. Now, you have to pour the water out of the glass into the spaces between the letters and every one has to contain the same amount— whatever its shape. Now try!'

That was it; letters are quantities, and spaces are quantities, and only the eye and the hand can measure them. As in the ear and the sensibilities of the poet sounds and syllables and pauses are quantities, so in both cases are the balancing and forward movement of these quantities only a matter of skill and feeling and art.

Ben Shahn

Someone wants you to make a poster. You are likely to be given a lot of scribbled information on a scrap of paper. From this, you have to work out a design which will make a strong visual impact and communicate the information clearly. It takes time and careful planning to make a good poster. In the first place you have to construct an appropriate *shape* and *size* of letter and simplify any other shapes that have to be included. Then these letters must be so arranged that the shapes *between* the letters and the words *balance* in a pleasing way within the shape of the whole poster. Not only must they balance but the message of the poster must make a clear impact from a distance. In fact

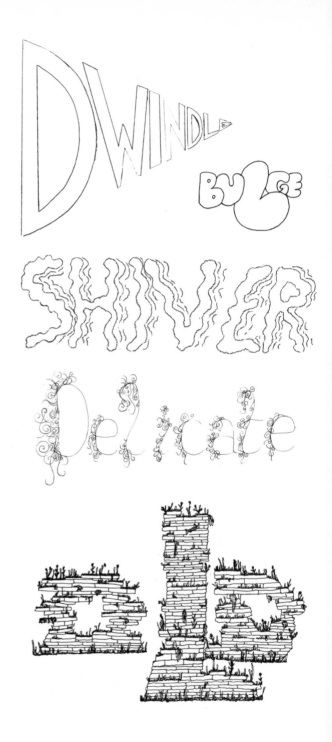

120

you must be able to have an overall view of your design. This is only possible if you work on the floor; then you can stand up and walk round to see the arrangement from several points of view.

1 Begin by reducing the words to a minimum. Leave out everything except the few essential words needed to give the right information.
2 Decide which words need the largest, fattest letters and which can be smaller.
3 Choose two sheets of coloured paper, one for the background and one for the letters. They must make a clear light and dark contrast so that the words can be read easily from a distance.
4 If it is necessary to include an object or a person, then you must turn these into simple shapes with a clear silhouette which can easily be identified (see page 33). Plan this shape *with* the letters so that all the shapes belong together.
5 Cut a long strip of coloured paper to the height of the letters you want to use. This might be 1in, 2in or 3in. Draw the letters on this so that they touch the top and bottom of the strip : $\frac{3}{4}$ to $\frac{1}{2}$in is a good width to use.
6 Cut the letters out. Now you can easily move them around until the arrangement feels right. Walk round and look at the shapes on the poster from another position. This will help you to see them as an abstract pattern on the page.
7 When you are satisfied that the shapes are well balanced, and the message of the poster is clear, mark the positions in pencil and using a thin layer of gum stick the letters down. The great advantage of this method is that should you need several copies of the same poster all you need to do is to draw round the cut out letters before you stick them down.

Opposite
Letter shapes that actually *look* like the meaning of the word. (14)

Above right
Poster for a party. Coloured inks and metallic paper. (18)

Right
Poster made with cut-out paper letters.

Christmas and birthday cards

drawing and painting materials
coloured papers
white card/poster board
coloured tissue paper
cow gum/rubber cement
lino-printing equipment (*pages* 131–2)

There are many occasions when we want to send someone a special kind of greeting. Shops offer us an enormous range of mass-produced cards but it is often difficult to find one that is really appropriate for the particular person who will receive it.

Instead of spending money on commercial cards, you could make your own. Everyone is pleased and flattered to receive a card that has been made specially for them. Certainly any hand-made individually designed card gives far more pleasure than the mass-produced ones. Try out some of the following suggestions and think up other ideas of your own.

1 Collect flowers, and press and arrange them on a piece of white card.
2 Fill a card completely with your greeting. Use large letter shapes that can be decorated with coloured felt-tip pens.
3 Choose a special subject that interests a friend, and collect relevant bits and pieces and photographs from magazines to make a collage card for his birthday.
4 Think of shapes that would be appropriate for special occasions, e.g. Halloween, Christmas, St Valentine's Day, Easter, Midsummer Day and anniversaries. Cut these out of card and decorate with coloured patterns.
5 Boil an egg hard, and while the shell is still warm paint patterns on it with coloured inks and give it as an Easter present.
6 Cut a design in lino (see page 132) and print your own cards on coloured tissue paper mounted on to white card/poster board.
7 Try a 'multiple' card in which each member of the family adds his own contribution to one of the sections, in a long concertina shape.

Designs for Christmas cards. Lino/linoleum, cut paper, and pressed flowers.

Programmes and invitations

white paper or card/poster board
pencils
ruler
pen and black drawing ink
'Letraset'

A local event in your town, or a special occasion at school, may give you an opportunity to design an invitation card or a programme. It is important that this should be done well. A lot of thought and effort is required to produce a good play and the programme should also reflect careful planning. Here are some suggestions to help you.

1 Decide on an appropriate *size* and *shape*. Invitation cards have to fit into a standard-size envelope. Programmes will be cut from standard sheets of paper so work out an economical proportion.

2 Choose the *colour* and *texture* of the paper or card. Hand-printing requires a soft, absorbent surface but a professional printer can use a wider range.

3 A lino-block (see page 132) is most suitable for printing cards and programmes and can be hand- or machine-printed. If you need a very detailed picture then you must make a drawing in black ink on white paper which will be printed professionally. Think about the letter shapes and the picture *together*. Turn your design upside down so that you can see it as an abstract pattern. Look past the letters at the spaces around them, new shapes carved out of the background by the letters themselves. This is hard to do. Screw up your eyes so that the shapes are accentuated or prop the design up and get a little distance away. This will help you to see it freshly and with a more critical eye.

4 The text inside the programme must also be considered as an abstract pattern on the page. To achieve this you will have to look at the length of words and sentences and make a plan of how all these long and short lengths will balance within the page. This a real puzzle but worth trying and it will certainly help you to understand the job of the typographer and printer. You may think words just automatically make themselves into a well-balanced design on the page. If you experiment a little you will see how untrue this is.

A fascinating thing to try is 'Letraset'. These are letter forms of different shapes and sizes which you can buy as complete sheets. They are adhesive and can be pressed or rubbed into position according to the plan you have made.

If not many copies are needed, a hand-printed linocut can be used for the cover, and the text reproduced on a Xerox or other duplicating machine, and added afterwards. The alternative is to consult a local printer, for unlike most things in modern life, a piece of printing can be personally commissioned and made to order. This is remarkable when you think that practically all our possessions are the result of mechanical mass production and there is no question of anyone asking our opinion about the design—we just have to accept it.

I suggest that you work out your ideas; think about size, shape, paper and colour and how much money you can spend, then visit a printer and ask his advice. With his collaboration you will have the pleasure of seeing how your first ideas can gradually grow into their final printed form. I can recommend the moment of unwrapping the printer's parcel, smelling the fresh printing ink and seeing several hundred copies of your design ready to be sent as invitation cards or handed out as programmes.

As you get older you may find other opportunities for commissioning special pieces of printing and collaborating in their design. This may be a letterhead, a brochure, a prospectus, a handbill or a menu-card: whatever it is, remember that it is up to you to work out your own ideas in a positive and *visual* way.

Look around and begin to build up a collection of any pieces of well designed printing that you see.

Make your own book

Choose an illustrated book that you specially enjoy looking at and think about the way it has been designed. Some pictures will fill a whole page and even go completely off the edges, others will occupy half a page or a chapter heading or make a decorative tailpiece to finish a chapter. The pages may have words arranged in two columns or they may go right across or even mingle with the pictures.

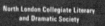

Opposite
Designs made for various programmes, tickets, and invitation cards.

Below
Cover and pages from a cookery book. Friends and parents provided the recipes and a group of young people, 10-18, made the illustrations.

Before you can decide about the arrangement of your book you must choose a subject and an appropriate size. You may be able to get a plain paper notebook that is the size you want to use. If not, the alternative is to cut paper to size and stitch it through the seams or to use a loose-leaf file so that pages can be added as the book grows.

You can make a book by yourself or collaborate with your family and friends.

Here are some possible themes to start you thinking:

a A story of your own, illustrated with your drawings. This might be for a younger brother or sister.
b A book about animals, trains, buildings or any subject that really interests you.
c A guide to the district in which you live.
d A 'collector's book' with drawings and photographs of things that you collect and, where possible, the objects themselves, e.g. match-box labels, stamps, shells, stones, flowers.
e A cookery book with your own drawings of food and cooking equipment and recipes from your family and friends.
f A *Heads, Bodies and Legs* book.
g An alphabet book.

Above
A group of ten friends aged 14 made this children's book where the heads, bodies and legs are interchangeable. Each figure is made of cut-paper shapes pasted onto a background. The shapes were cut from a variety of textures and patterns found in magazines, newspapers and a wallpaper sample book. Added to these are textured papers made by hand.

Right
Cowboy from *Heads, Bodies and Legs.* The lines indicate where the page should be cut.

Your school magazine

Have you ever thought about your school magazine? It probably appears each year and provides everyone with a record of events, including some selected pieces of writing. But apart from this there is the opportunity to make a magazine that is really worth *looking* at. I don't mean the addition of a few odd drawings and linocuts fitted in at random, but a real integration of text and pictures so that the whole magazine is a delight to the eye. Obviously this needs careful planning and good places for decoration are the front and back covers, end papers, title page, headings, frontispiece, centre page and tailpieces. If there is to be a special theme in a magazine, this could provide the opportunity for stimulating visual ideas. Advertisement pages need not remain dull mass-produced material that is repeated in hundreds of other magazines. Instead, these could be redesigned especially for your own magazine. Your editor would need the advertisers' approval but a new approach would probably be welcomed by them.

Certainly some schools are already producing magazines that are taking advantage of all these exciting possibilities and their productions have become collector's pieces. But there are still far too many dull and dreary ones that have missed the opportunity altogether. Sometimes this is true of schools where a visit to the art room reveals a marvellous exhibition of drawings and paintings. There is no reason why art should be confined within studios. We do need to spend time studying the language of art but our discoveries should be used to enrich our lives in all kinds of ways. I hope that within your own school community you will find the chance not only to illustrate the magazine but also to design murals, scenery, costumes, posters, invitation cards and programmes.

Two covers of school magazines and pages with lino-cuts illustrating the theme of 'London'.

Print-making

You have already tried one kind of printing when you made rubbings to find out more about texture (page 55). Each method has its own particular characteristics which you will discover while you are working. This element of exploration is one of the rewarding qualities in print-making. The process carries you along and helps you, in a very direct way, to find out more about the language of art.

As usual, it is best to avoid having preconceived ideas about what you expect to happen. I think the most important thing about any of the methods is to *watch* what is happening at each stage of the printing. By doing this all kinds of ideas will occur to you about combinations of colour and texture, the arrangement of shapes, and ways of adapting your ideas in a new direction.

The surfaces that you print from each have their own character as do the various papers that you print on. These surfaces and paper qualities determine the nature of the final print. Thin, absorbent paper gives a different result from the same block printed on thicker, less absorbent paper. Hand-printing has the advantage of allowing your fingers control over pressure. Therefore the ink can be pressed lightly or firmly into the paper and different textures can be achieved.

Before you begin any kind of printing, a certain amount of preparation is essential. Always cover the table with overlapping sheets of newspaper and arrange your equipment in an orderly way. Cut your paper into a convenient size *before* you start to print, and decide where to put the wet prints. You may have a pin-up board in your room, and this would be ideal. If not, you could fix a string across the room and hang your prints up with pegs. Prints that are not wet and sticky could be spread out on another table or put temporarily on the floor.

The methods described in this section will help you to begin. After that, you can go on and find new ways for yourself.

Frottage

sheets of sugar paper/construction paper or thin card/ poster board
firm card/poster board or hardboard
scissors
p.v.a. glue
wax crayons

A method of making rubbings or *frottage* is described on pages 55–6. As well as taking rubbings from man-made reliefs and natural forms, it is possible to take them from raised surfaces you have made yourself.

1 Cut a piece of card, about 10 x 8in, for a base.
2 Then cut a piece of sugar paper or thin card to about the same size as the base. Using scissors, without preliminary pencil lines, divide the paper into a few simple geometrical shapes.
3 Arrange these shapes on the base. Aim to make satisfying new shapes in the spaces between.
4 Mark the position of the pieces and stick them down.
5 When the glue is dry, cover your design with a sheet of thin paper. Hold it down firmly and rub across the surface with a wax crayon. Try different pressures and directions to and see what happens.

You can take more rubbings from the 'block' using two or more colours.

Experiment with other designs. You could cut a bird or animal out of paper and add *texture* by glueing smaller

Opposite top left
Bird in a tree. Paper shapes glued on to card/poster board.

Opposite top right
Wax rubbing taken from the raised surface. (11)

Opposite
Mole. Print taken from a picture made by glueing string to card. (13)

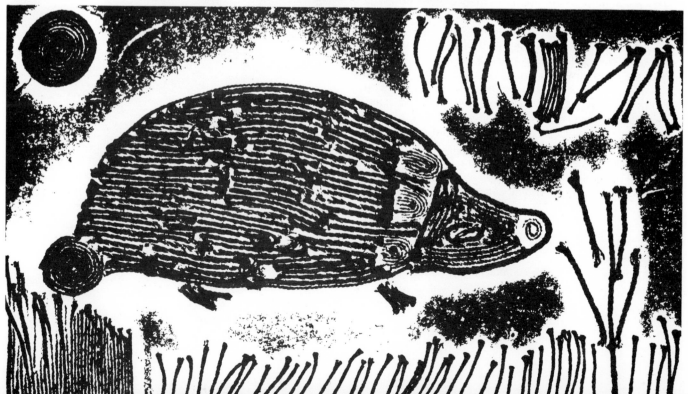

pieces on top of the main shape. Besides paper shapes, pieces of textured fabrics can be glued down and *lines* added by using pieces of string.

Collect other bits and pieces and try combining them together on a base of thick card or hardboard, e.g. sandpaper, paper doyleys, lace cloth, scraps of metal mesh, corrugated card, textured chocolate box wrappings, hessian and aluminium foil. Aim to build up a design with a rich variety of contrasting textures.

Stencils

cartridge paper/drawing paper
scissors or sharp knife
crayons and powder paint
coloured inks

This is another way of printing with cut paper shapes. Instead of using the surface of the shape, you can use the space *inside* the shape. This becomes a 'stencil' through which colour can be applied to a background.

1 On a piece of cartridge paper about 12 x 10in, draw the shape of a fish or any object with a simple silhouette.
2 Cut this out carefully, using scissors or a sharp knife. If you use a knife, put a thick piece of cardboard under the paper to avoid damaging the table.
3 Put the stencil down on another piece of paper. Choose a method for applying colour through the shape. You could use crayons, paint or coloured ink. The paint needs to be mixed dryly and stippled on with a bristle brush. Ink or paint could also be stippled on with an ink pad. This is made by wrapping some cotton wool tightly in a cloth and tying it at the top. Another method is to roll printing ink across the paper. This will make a flat, silhouette shape which can now be overprinted with a second colour.
4 Remove the stencil. Use the paper shape which was cut out originally and remove enough pieces to leave

Top right
Swan. Dryish powder paint stippled through a paper stencil. (13)

Right
Tortoise. Coloured ink stippled through a paper stencil using a cloth pad. (13)

130

an interesting set of shapes for a second colour. For instance from a fish shape you could cut out a pattern of scales, fins and an eye. Put this new stencil over the first shape and colour through the spaces.

By experimenting you can discover many other ways of cutting and printing with stencils.

Lino printing

In this method the design is made by cutting away parts of the surface of the block. The raised surface prints *black* and the cut away lines and shapes reveal *white*. We are going to work with lino-blocks but you could also use wood or hardboard. You need good quality lino with a plain matt surface. This can be bought from an art shop, or sometimes from a local furnishing department. The colour is usually brown and I suggest that you rub over the surface

Below
Cutting a lino-block.

Top right
A print from a block exploring some of the lines and textural marks that can be made with a cutting tool. (16)

Bottom right
The rider. A complicated subject has been described in a simple way by carefully selecting just the necessary white lines to cut from the black block. (14)

with black Indian ink or gouache. This will help you to see the lines made by the cutting tool.

Cutting tools can be either the kind with fixed handles, or the ones with removable nibs. The most useful sizes are the No. 1 and 2 v-shaped cutters, and No. 8 u-shaped gouge.

For printing you will need:

a 3 or 4in roller
plate-glass slab or formica-topped board about 10 x 8in
palette knife for mixing colours
tubes of oil or water-based printing ink (black, white, red, blue and yellow are the basic colours, and these can be mixed to make other colours)
turpentine for cleaning oil-based inks
plenty of soft rags, paper tissues and newspapers

Prepare your table for printing as described above.

Take a piece of lino, about 8 x 8in, and hold it firmly on the table with one hand. Grasp the lino tool in the palm of your other hand and practise cutting lines from one side of the block to the other. Begin with a No. 2 tool. *Make sure that the hand holding the lino is always behind the cutting tool* to avoid cutting yourself if the tool slips. Watch the shape of the line as the lino curls up in front of your tool. When you stop cutting you should have a heap of these lino 'lines'. The uncut block would print as a square of black velvet so every line you cut is a *white* line. Experiment with different thicknesses and directions of line. Try some straight lines, some curving and some that begin thin and gradually thicken.

Try using the tools in other ways. The u-shaped tool removes larger areas of lino. All the tools can make a variety of marks which suggest different *textures*. Experiment to see what textures you can make.

Shake the block to remove all the loose pieces. Clear away all the lino debris from the table to prevent stray bits getting into the printing ink.

Preparation for printing
Cut up paper into right size, i.e. several inches larger than the printing block. Any soft absorbent paper will do. Newsprint and tissue paper are cheap and suitable. Avoid paper with a hard, shiny surface.

Arrange the printing materials in a logical order on your table. Keep the rolling-up area separate from the printing

Woman in a chair. Drawing with a lino tool using lines, shapes, textures, and patterns. (18)

area. When the printing table gets messy, replace the dirty newspaper with clean paper. Keep a rag handy to wipe your fingers.

1 Squeeze about 1in of ink on to the slab and roll it out until you have spread the ink evenly on the roller and the slab. Then roll up the block in all directions until the whole surface is evenly inked.

2 Turn the block over and lower it gently on to the printing paper. Press it down firmly.

3 Put your hand under the paper and the block and turn them both face upwards. Rub across the surface of the block and feel the lines and textures with your fingers. Press the paper firmly along all four edges. Lift up a corner to see if you have pressed hard enough. If you need more pressure put the paper back in position and go on rubbing. Pressure can also be applied with the back of a spoon or a clean roller.
4 Peel the paper away and pin the print up to dry. You can see the character of the lines and textures which you have cut.

Lino-cutting is a method of drawing which is rather like working with white paint on black paper. Now see if you can make a drawing directly on to another piece of lino using only the cutting tools. You will need to resist the temptation to draw first in pencil. If you can do this you will learn a lot about the character of this new material and how to use it. You could support the lino block on a firm board and make a drawing from your window or of someone sitting in the room.

Lino is an ideal material to use for all kinds of work. You could use it for making programmes and Christmas cards. You might also plan your own book and illustrate it with linocuts.

When you have finished printing, the roller, the inking slab and the block must be thoroughly cleaned with turpentine. Any ink left will harden and stick permanently.

Lino/linoleum printing in colour

This is a method for making colour prints where you only need to use one block for all the colours. The first colour printed should be light in tone as it will be a base for all the other colours printed over it.

1 Squeeze out about 1in white printing ink and add only a tiny amount of other colours and mix together with a palette knife.
2 Roll out evenly on the printing slab and then roll up an uncut lino-block about 9 x 9in.
3 Print this block on at least six sheets of paper. This is the 'base' colour which underlies all the following colours.
4 Clean the block and cut out your first lines.

Public house. Only one lino block has been used and cut in an elimination sequence to make this three-colour print. 12 × 18in. (16)

5 Mix another colour, slightly darker than the first. Roll up the block thinly and print it on top of each of the previous prints by registering corner to corner.
6 Clean the block again and cut away more lino.
7 Mix another colour and print the block over the previous two colours. It is not necessary to wait for the prints to dry before over-printing.
8 Go on cutting the block and printing layer over layer until you have just enough lino left to print the final colour.
9 Clean everything carefully.

Many artists, including Picasso, have used this intriguing method. Once you have tried it yourself, you will understand how it could be used to develop other ideas suggested in this book.

Prints from cardboard

firm white card/poster board about ⅛in thick
sharp, 'handyman's' knife and steel ruler

We have seen how cardboard can be used to build up surfaces for making rubbings. It can also be rolled up with printing ink in the same way as a lino block. For cutting you must have a really good knife and preferably a steel ruler as the blade may cut into a wooden one.

1 Begin by using a small piece of card about 12 x 10in. With a ruler and pencil divide the rectangle into three or four simple shapes that could be easily pulled apart and slotted together again.
2 Put another larger piece of card underneath to protect the table. Hold the ruler very firmly and cut carefully along each line several times until you feel the blade touching the cardboard underneath.
3 Slide the pieces apart; put them on a sheet of white paper and try out various ways of relating them together. Watch the new shapes being made by the *spaces* in between. Choose an arrangement and mark the position of the pieces in pencil.
4 Remove one piece at a time, roll up with printing ink and return it to the marked position. You can, if you like, use a different colour for each shape.
5 Gently lower a sheet of printing paper over the surface:

Above
Print taken from a cardboard rectangle cut into six shapes and opened out to reveal new shapes in the background spaces. (18)

Opposite
House in the country. Print taken from a variety of card shapes made with a guillotine, hole punch, and scissors. 13 × 15in (14)

press down and rub firmly. Peel the paper away and pin the print up to dry. Move the shapes and try out new arrangements.

Monoprints

This is a method of printing from a completely flat surface. A piece of plate glass makes a good, smooth surface but you could use a sheet of metal, perspex or a formica-topped board. This is rolled up with a thin layer of printing ink in the same way as a lino-block. Any marks made on the surface of the ink can be printed on to paper. The word 'monoprint' derives from the fact that you are only able to take one print from each design.

There are all kinds of ways of using this process. Here are a few ideas to start you off, but you will find that each method can be adapted to other ways which will occur to you during the printing.

136

Direct working on the block

1 Squeeze out a little printing ink on to the glass and using a brush dipped in turpentine draw directly on the surface. You could add to the drawing by removing areas of ink with a soft rag.
2 Lower a sheet of paper over the drawing and press firmly with your fingers. Peel the paper away and pin the print up to dry.
3 You could try a variation of this method by using either coloured printing inks or oil paints. It is also worth experimenting with water-based inks and paints.

Line drawing

1 Squeeze out about ⅜in of black printing ink on to the glass and roll it out thinly and evenly across the whole surface.
2 Lower a sheet of paper very gently on to the inked slab but do not press it down.
3 Without touching the paper with your hand, use a pencil or pen to make a drawing on it.
4 Gently lift the paper off the glass. You will see that your drawing has printed as a black line on white. If the background has also printed, then you need to roll up the slab with a thinner layer of ink.

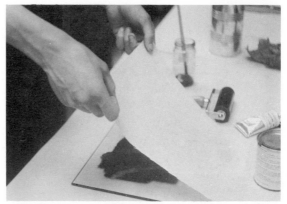

Masking

1 Roll up the slab evenly across the whole surface.
2 Use pieces of cut or torn paper to mask out areas. Think not only about the white paper shapes but also look at the black shapes in between.
3 Lower a piece of printing paper over the block and press firmly with your fingers.

This method can be used in combination with either of the other methods I have described. Experiment and see what you can do yourself.

Right

a. Drawing into the ink with turpentine.

b. Lowering paper on to the block.

c. Applying gentle pressure.

d. Taking the print.

Using three dimensions

Most of the ideas in this book are to do with working in two dimensions, but of course there are many ways of using your materials to make things in three dimensions. I described some of these on pages 60–68. At school you may be having pottery and woodwork classes and so you will be familiar with using clay and wood. As in printing, and all other methods, each material has its own special character which you can only really discover when you begin to use it.

In working with three dimensions, you will be thinking about the other basic elements in the language of art and using these to construct solid forms in space. Try out the suggestions in this section and adapt them to work in other ways that occur to you.

Above
Papier-mâché birds painted with gouache. (11)

Opposite
A collection of different shapes and sizes of empty boxes. Arranged together and sprayed with gold paint, they lose their separate identities and, like buildings in a city, combine to make a new three-dimensional form. Base 9 × 9in. (18)

Clay and papier-mâché

clay or plasticine
vaseline
newspapers
wallpaper paste
white card/poster board
scissors
powder paint or gouache

Here is a simple method of making three-dimensional forms.

1 Build up the egg-like shape of a bird's body, using plasticine if clay is not available. The wings and tail can be added later, so don't include them at this stage.

2 Tear up a page of newspaper into small pieces, about 1 x 1in. Use another page of contrasting colour or larger type-faces and tear this up into a separate pile of pieces.

3 Cover the clay with a thin layer of vaseline. Wet the paper pieces thoroughly by dipping them into wallpaper paste and cover the surface of the bird with about six overlapping layers of paper. Use the two heaps alternately so that you can see when you have completed each layer.

4 Leave overnight to dry in a warm place. Then cut in half with a sharp knife, remove the clay and stick the two halves together again with strips of newspaper soaked in paste. You could use sellotape but this is more difficult to paint over.

5 Cut two wings and a tail out of thin card and stick these to the body in a similar way. Now the bird is ready to be decorated with colours and patterns.

Think about other simple forms that could be made with this method and try them out for yourself. For example, you could blow up a balloon and use this as a base instead of clay. This spherical head-like shape makes an excellent beginning for a mask.

Mobiles

thin cane dowelling or wire
nylon thread
white card/poster board
scissors

Mobiles are aerial sculpture. Shapes, lines and colours can be made to hang and move in space. You will need to experiment to find methods of hanging the pieces so that they relate together and turn and twist in a satisfying way.

1 Cut out a variety of cardboard shapes. You could use squares, triangles and circles or the silhouette shapes of birds and fish decorated with a pattern on both sides.
2 Balance a piece of thin cane, dowelling or wire by hanging it from a thread tied round the centre.
3 Hang other shorter pieces of the same material from the ends of this so that they move about easily.
4 Try hanging some of your shapes from the smaller pieces and see if you can find the correct position of balance for each one.
5 Use some other things, e.g. coloured Christmas tree balls, corks, buttons, etc. Notice how different weights and lengths of thread make different kinds of movement. Experiment by tying the string nearer one end of the main piece of cane instead of in the middle and put more weight on the shorter side, like balancing a see-saw.
6 Fix the finished mobile to hang at a height and in a position where it will spin and make the most interesting movements.

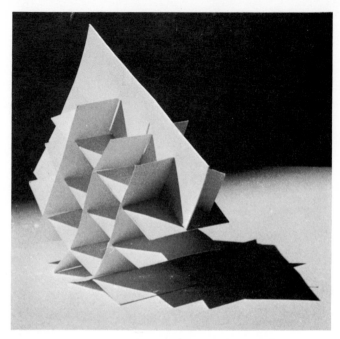

Above
Construction using white card. Notice how the form is enriched by the pattern of light and dark tones. Height 5in. (15)

Opposite left
Mobile with decorated cardboard shapes representing weather symbols. (15)

Opposite right
A precarious balance of scraps of wood and nails makes this unusual mobile. (14)

Cardboard construction

strips of white card/poster board about 2in wide
scissors
ruler

Another way of building a construction in space is with strips of cardboard.

1 Cut a piece of white card into strips of equal width.
2 Divide the strips into various lengths.

3 Cut into them carefully up to half their width to make slots which can join them together.
4 Try out various ways of arranging the pieces so that you build up a structure without using glue. You could vary this method of construction by using strips of different widths.

Turn the construction round and look at it from various points of view. If necessary, add more pieces of card. Cut out a base for the construction to stand on. Try making drawings of your construction from two different positions.

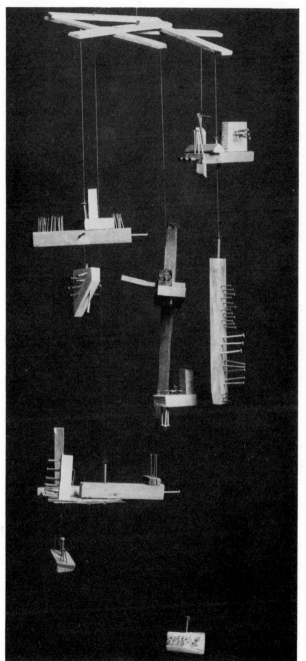

Left
Scraps of wood assembled to make a structure of shapes and tones. Notice the counterchange rhythm of squares and circles on the right hand side. (16)

A personal totem

three-dimensional junk
p.v.a. glue
white paint

Everything that you make is to do with yourself. You have seen that the language of art is as much a personal means of expression as is the language of writing and speaking. If you have been following the suggestions in this book you will have discovered all kinds of starting points for developing your own ideas. In this final section I suggest that you think out a way of making your own personal 'totem'.

This is the name given to the large wooden sculptures made by the Indian tribes living along the N.W. coast of America. Usually carved from a single tree trunk they were placed in front of each house in the village as a symbolic representation of the occupant. In a similar way we use heraldic crests to represent families.

At the seaside, or in the country, you may come across an old chunk of wood that might be suitable for a totem. The carving opposite was made from a piece of driftwood which seemed to contain in itself the suggestion of a figure. A chisel was used to define the features and a line was cut away to suggest the division between the upper and lower portions of the body.

Another kind of totem is seen opposite. This structure was designed to commemorate the artist Piet Mondrian: the chosen colours and shapes reflect the character of his abstract paintings.

Think about the totem that you might put together for yourself.

1 Collect a heap of three-dimensional junk: empty boxes, cardboard cylinders, plastic containers, egg-boxes, apple trays, polystyrene packaging—in fact anything that you can find. Pick out the objects that are most interesting to handle and give them a coat of white emulsion paint. This will help you to see their

Wooden assemblage

scrap pieces of wood
a firm base
glue
knife and sandpaper

A chunky solid construction can be made from wood: you could get small scraps or off-cuts from a local woodyard.

1 Use a strong piece of wood for a base and try out different arrangements of the pieces. Turn the base round so that you can look at the construction from other angles.
2 Go on moving the pieces about until the *total shape* of the whole arrangement is satisfying from all points of view. If necessary, adjust the shape or size of the pieces with a knife or sandpaper.
3 Stick everything down with p.v.a. glue.

If you have a camera you will find that this kind of three-dimensional assemblage can be fascinating to photograph. Look through the viewfinder and study the balance of light and dark tones that you see. Now move into another position where the light affects the structure in a different way. Take photographs to record the changes.

Below
Carving from a chunk of driftwood. Height 3ft. (17)

Right
Painting a personal totem made from discarded junk. (13)

Below right
Eduardo Paolozzi: City of the Circle and the Square.
1963, acrylic paint on metal, 83 × 40¼ × 26¼in. Tate Gallery.

form and to forget that the cylinder was originally a container for scouring powder and the box a detergent packet.

2 Now assemble the objects together and aim to build up a giant sculpture larger than yourself. Be prepared to experiment. Add or take away pieces and, if appropriate, enrich the surfaces with colour and pattern. There is no ready made answer. It is up to you to explore the possibilities.

Looking at art

One never finishes learning about art. There are always new things to discover. Great works of art seem to look different each time one stands before them. They seem to be as inexhaustible and unpredictable as real human beings. It is an exciting world of its own with its own strange laws and its own adventures.

E. H. Gombrich

Finally, apart from developing our own ideas and our own creative work, we need to extend our experience by studying the work of great artists. It is really impossible to put into words the feelings we have when we look at a work of art because in looking we become involved in a special kind of *encounter.* Unlike our meetings with people, there is no exchange of words but a silent dialogue between the work of art and ourselves. Certainly it is true that, as with people, there are some encounters which prove immediately pleasing while others are less successful, but it is equally true that both people and works of art may need time for us to get to know them better and appreciate them properly.

First of all we should remember that artists are not all aiming to achieve the same result. By trying out some of the ideas in this book you yourself know that art is a language that can be used in many ways. Some people make the mistake of thinking that an artist has only succeeded if the people or objects in the picture look 'real'. If you asked them what they meant by 'real' they might admit that they want to see something instantly recognizable as a faithful copy of the original. A few artists have been preoccupied with this kind of illusionism but you need only turn the pages of a book about the history of art to understand at once that the world of art reflects a vast range of ideas and attitudes about reality.

When we look at works of art we need to ask ourselves what these ideas were; what the artist was aiming to express; and how he achieves his purpose. For instance, he may be aiming to describe a particular aspect of the *appearance* of things: he may be expressing his *feelings* about what he sees, or trying to investigate the hidden *structure* that underlies the surface appearance. You will see work by artists with other aims but these three attitudes can be recognized throughout the history of art. To understand this more clearly, I suggest that you begin by looking at the paintings of Monet, Van Gogh and Cézanne.

Claude Monet was a Frenchman working in the second half of the last century. He was concerned with taking a whole new look at the appearance of things. He worked hard to train his eyes to record the way in which *light* influences colour. An example of this can be seen in a series of his paintings of the front of Rouen Cathedral. Although they all have the same subject, they look quite different from each other because each one was painted at a different time of the day. We know a cathedral is made of stone but through the eyes of Monet we see how it can be transformed by light into patches of glowing colour. Painters like Constable and Turner can open our eyes in a similar way.

Painting at the same time as Monet was a young Dutchman called Vincent van Gogh. He was equally absorbed in experimenting with the use of colour but he used it to express his own inner thoughts and feelings about the things that he painted (see page 20).

Yet another approach was being explored by Paul Cézanne. Unlike Monet, he aimed to look beyond the mere appearance of things to something far more fundamental. He worked to analyse the underlying structure that lies behind our visual world. By probing into the nature of reality, Cézanne helped other artists to experiment further.

Some became less concerned to represent a subject in their paintings. They began to express their ideas directly through shapes, forms and colours and to paint abstract pictures, that is pictures where the shapes are no longer the equivalent for objects and people.

Without a 'subject' to look at, you may ask, 'What is the

Above
Paul Cézanne: Rocky Landscape, Aix.
1885, oil on canvas, 25 × 31¼in, National Gallery, London.
There are many different ways of looking at landscape. Here the artist has chosen colours and shapes to analyse and reconstruct what he understands about its chunky three-dimensional qualities.

Right
Joan Miro: Woman and Bird in the Moonlight.
1949, oil on canvas, Tate Gallery, London.
This is a painting where the artist is concerned with an altogether different world from our everyday experience. The shapes, lines and colours look playfully back at us and, like poetry, challenge our imagination. © ADAGP Paris 1984.

painting about?' Well, it is about the same things that all paintings have in common. This is the expression of the artist's ideas through a visual language; his ability to select and organize shapes and to manipulate qualities like balance and rhythm, and elements like colour and texture until he achieves the result he is searching for. This search for a *visual structure* is the basis of all works of art of whatever period whether they represent a subject or use entirely abstract forms. If you are willing to pause and look for this underlying structure you will find that abstract art will speak to you very directly in a similar way to music.

Other artists continued to use objects in their paintings but only to provide them with a starting point for exploring

new visual ideas. You can see how Braque used some objects on a table and selected from them the basic elements that he found most interesting. For him, these were the flat shapes and colours that could be organized together into a new arrangement (page 34). A starting point of objects, or people, or landscapes, led other great innovators, like Picasso, in quite different directions (pages 151 and 155).

One group, which came to be known as the 'Surrealists' were involved in searching for ways of expressing ideas that lie hidden deep in our subconscious minds. This is the part of ourselves that we know a little about through dreams rather than through straightforward reasoning. In their paintings Max Ernst, Joan Miro and Paul Klee explored this strange visual world that is startlingly

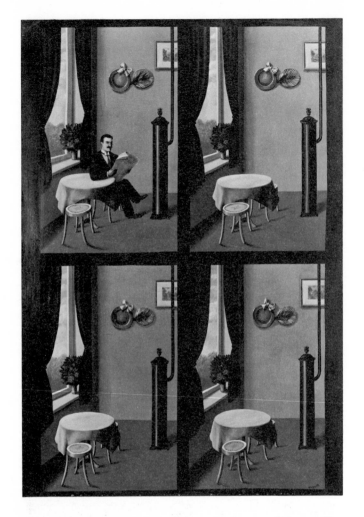

Jackson Pollock, later labelled as an 'Action Painter', experimented by spreading his canvas on the floor and applying paint by 'dipping a small house brush, stick or trowel into a tin, and then by rapid movements of the wrist, arm or body, quickly allowing it to fall in weaving rhythms over the surface'. This unorthodox method of working helped artists to explore the value of the accidental mark and spontaneous lines and rhythms.

While some artists become preoccupied with these tactile qualities of the paint surface, others have attempted to remove these qualities altogether. Painters like Frank Stella and Kenneth Noland reacted against the emotional expression of 'action painting' and became concerned with using flat areas of unbroken paint with hard clean edges.

Another line of investigation has been followed by artists interested in creating disturbing optical phenomena. Through the play of inverse patterns, black on white and white on black and at times the use of colours, the spectators' eyes are stimulated and involved in illusions of movement on a static, two-dimensional surface.

Movement itself has for some become an important point of inquiry. Mobiles and kinetic inventions by artists like Alexander Calder and J. R. Soto use a wide range of materials and break down the conventional divisions between painting and sculpture.

Another division that has been broken down is that between traditionally 'artistic' subject-matter and the commercial art that surrounds us in daily life. 'Pop' artists have developed their ideas from popular images that are familiar to us all. Roy Lichtenstein uses the strong, linear structure of comic strip cartoons and Tom Wesselmann, another American artist, combines paint, photographs, reproductions, advertising images, and actual three-dimensional objects together in one picture.

Ideas are changing and developing, not only through the experience of the artist but also through vast scientific advances. Electron microscopes reveal a strange world hidden to our normal eyes ; giant telescopes study unknown areas of the universe and astronauts send us televison pictures from space. Both the artist and the scientist are free to explore in many directions. From the past and today you yourself will encounter a rich variety of things to look at and enjoy. Keep an open mind and you will discover how all these ideas can enrich your own imagination.

different from our everyday experience. Others, like Dali and Magritte, painted everyday objects with a meticulous attention to detail and used incongruous relationships and scale to produce a kind of truth we all recognize as a form of reality.

Characteristic of the art of the last twenty years are new attitudes to the use of scale, materials and methods. Many artists have rejected the popular 'easel' picture of a size suitable to hang in a small room and have worked on enormous canvases making a powerful impact and involving the spectator in a new experience.

146

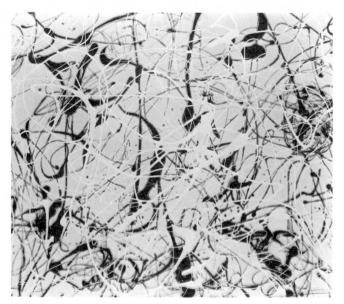

Opposite
Rene Magritte: L'Homme au Journal. © ADAGP Paris 1984.
1927, oil on canvas, 32 × 45½in, Tate Gallery, London.
Why should the near repetition be so fascinating? Perhaps the
man in the first picture will return: perhaps, as in a film sequence,
something else is about to happen?

Above
Jackson Pollock: Number 23.
1948, enamel paint on board, 22 × 30in. Tate Gallery, London.
A spontaneous use of paint dripped and swirled across a canvas
laid flat on the floor. These lines and marks have an intensely
personal energy reflecting the artist's physical involvement and his
capacity for seizing powerful structures in apparently random
effects.

Above right
Roy Lichtenstein: Detail of 'Whaam!'
1963, acrylic paint on canvas, 68 × 160in, Tate Gallery, London.
Paintings can have all kinds of starting points. Here the artist is
using the 'popular art' of the strip cartoon. The tiny original is
greatly enlarged and subtly redesigned on a new scale.

Right
Frank Stella: Hyena Stomp.
1962, acrylic paint on canvas, 77 × 77in. Tate Gallery, London.
A precisely calculated design based on a rectangular spiral divided
into four sections. This artist is using a 'hard-edge', coolly
detached approach quite unlike that of Pollock.

Tipu's Tiger.
1790, painted wood, Victoria and Albert Museum, London.
A wooden carving representing a royal tiger in the act of devouring
a European. Inside the tiger is a miniature organ and, when a
handle is turned, this produces tiger-like roars and sounds
resembling the cries of a person in distress. While the organ is
playing, the man's left arm moves up and down to express his
helpless condition. The model was made for the amusement of
Tipu, Sultan of Mysore.

Visiting galleries and museums

Reproductions of works of art are pleasing to look at but
it is far more exciting to stand in front of the real thing.
You can feel the texture of the materials and imagine the
artist actually making the lines and brush strokes. This is
particularly true if you yourself have used materials in a
similar way. Your own attempts will have helped you
to be more appreciative of the work that you are looking
at. For instance, if you enjoy drawing with pen and ink,
using transparent watercolour or thick opaque paint, go
and look at the different ways in which other artists have
used the same material. In looking at the original you can
also see the real size of the work. Reproductions often
give us the wrong feeling of scale; tiny pictures, in a book,
in reality may be huge paintings on a canvas 9 x 12ft.

Carlo Crivelli: The Annunciation.
1486, $57\frac{3}{4} \times 81\frac{1}{2}$in, National Gallery, London.
A painting where the artist is clearly concerned with exploring the
laws of mathematical perspective to create an illusion of three
dimensions. See if you can find the point on the horizon where all
the parallel lines vanish.

Opposite
A detail from the painting above. If you look carefully you will
see that there are many tiny pictures like this contained within the
larger one.

The best way to get to know pictures is to go back again and again to look at the same ones. In this way you learn more than if you walk around trying to look briefly at everything. Galleries and museums can be overwhelming. There is so much to look at that we can easily wander aimlessly around without seeing anything properly. Try looking for particular things and this will help you to see. Here are some suggestions.

1 If you could take a painting home, which one would you choose?

2 Find paintings which show that the artist is particularly interested in:
a the arrangement of *flat shapes*
b the expression of a *mood* or feeling
c the use of materials to show *texture*
d creating the illusion of *space*.

3 Look for paintings where the artist has based his ideas on a theme that interests you: maybe a subject that you yourself have tried. See if you can understand what his intentions were and try to imagine how he set about

Study of a Greek pot. Pencil on cartridge paper. (12)

solving the problems that were involved. In this way you will begin to see the mind of the artist at work.

Look around in a similar way when you visit a museum. Choose a subject and see how it has been translated into various materials. You can look for example for *flowers* or *birds* and find how different they look when they are woven into *tapestry*, carved in *wood* and painted on *pottery*. Use your sketchbook to make simple line drawings of what you see. This will help you to look properly and you will remember much more than if you just walk around with no purpose.

If you travel in your own country or abroad, look not only at galleries and museums but also at churches, cathedrals and great houses. Walk about until you get a real feeling of where you are. Look under your feet where you may see the patterns of tiles or the textures of worn pavements. Look up above your head for carvings that are hidden away and for the rich, glowing colours of stained glass. Postcards are a good record of such visits, but look purposefully around you for details that the postcard photographer has completely missed.

150

Picasso : Painter and knitting model, 1927, etching.

Study a painting

A picture is not thought out and settled beforehand. While it is being done it changes, one's thoughts change. And when it is finished, it still goes on changing, according to the state of mind of whoever is looking at it. A picture lives a life like a living creature, undergoing changes imposed on us by our life from day to day. This is natural enough, as the picture lives only through the man who is looking at it.

Picasso

Paintings which represent something beautiful, with which we are familiar, are the easiest for us to appreciate. Horses grazing in a field, a brilliant sunset, a bowl of flowers: all these have an immediate visual impact because of their subject matter and the association of pleasant thoughts. Without this familiar link of easily appreciated subject matter, we may glance at a painting and walk away. In fact we are not allowing ourselves to look at all. We are blinded by our own preconceived ideas of what is, and what is not, acceptable and beautiful.

Recently I watched a film called *Waves*, commissioned by BBC television from Patrick Carey. There was no spoken commentary and no background music; just a series of magnificent photographs of waves and the sound of water. For the first few minutes I found it was difficult

Van Brussel: Flowerpiece.
1792, oil on wood, 23⅛ × 32in, National Gallery, London.
Several friends studied a reproduction of this painting shown
enlarged through a slide projector. The picture was seen for
about fifteen minutes but no notes or drawings were made.
Without seeing it again, each person painted a picture from what
they remembered. Naturally most of the intricate detail was left
out and different areas selected for emphasis.
On the right you can see that the large white flower, the rose on
the table, and the birds' nest have been given special importance.
Although many of the flowers have not been included, those that
remain recall the rhythm of the tightly packed design which
occupied the painter of the original picture. Powder paint on
sugar paper. 15 × 22in. (12)

to concentrate because my mind is so conditioned to looking at images on the television screen accompanied by words and music. An effort of adjustment was needed for my eyes to be capable of just *looking*.

This same problem occurs when we try to look at paintings and other works of art. 'Tell me what it *means*', or 'What it is *supposed* to be?', we say. The number in the catalogue tells us the title, and perhaps adds some words for us to read, and this becomes a substitute for *seeing* the painting itself.

Picasso says that a painting lives only through the man who is looking at it. For real enjoyment and understanding of art, we ourselves must be prepared to pause, and observe, forgetting about the intervention of words. The message is not a verbal but a visual one. To make contact with the painting we need to get on to the right wavelength. Try to remember this the next time you are confronted with a work of art that does not have an immediate impact for you. There may be a code to unscramble and you must give your eyes time to adjust.

An interesting way of studying a painting is to visit a gallery to choose a picture that you enjoy looking at, and buy a postcard reproduction. Go back to the painting and compare the original with the reproduction. First of all you will be aware of the difference in size. The actual *scale* of a picture is, of course, very important. Large paintings make a strong impact which cannot be felt on the size of a postcard.

Then compare the *colour*. You will notice that the printed colours remind us of the original but are not quite the same. Apart from perhaps a blue being too mauvish, or a green too brownish, you will see that the reproduction cannot show the exact *texture* of the paint. We can only appreciate the substance of the materials that the artist has used when we look closely at the painting itself.

This also applies to sculpture. From a reproduction we know that the sculpture is made of stone, wood or metal, but only when we are close enough to touch the original can we really enjoy the actual material.

Look again at the postcard reproduction: turn it upside down so that your eyes are jolted into seeing the underlying structure of the design—the organization of *shape, colour* and *tone*. Walk a few paces away from the original painting and try to think why the artist has chosen those particular shapes and colours.

It might help you if you made a few diagrams in your sketchbook. In an empty gallery you should have no difficulty in doing this, though if there are other people around you may feel embarrassed at the idea of drawing. Once you have got over the first few moments of nervousness you will find it easier than you imagined. After all, what could be a more suitable place for drawing than an art gallery.

Aim to make simple diagrams to search out the important main shapes and look for the balance of light and dark tones. Invent your own colour code: choose words that will help you to think of a *particular* rather than a general colour. For instance, words like 'soft, marshmallow pink', or 'warm toasty brown' are more explicit than just 'pink' or 'brown'.

By now you will have begun to know your chosen painting much better. When you get home see if you can reconstruct the picture from memory with the aid of your notes but without the postcard reproduction. The original may have been painted in oil colours but there is no need for you to use identical materials or to paint on the same scale. It is only essential to work to the same *proportion*. Any materials could be used: gouache, crayons, collage and so on.

Naturally, what you do will not be an exact facsimile, or even very like the original. This does not matter. Rather in the way that you might reconstruct a story that you have heard, you inevitably add something of your own. The point is that you will have found out far more about your chosen painting than if you had just stood in front of it for a few moments. When you have time, go back to the gallery and look at the painting again. Your eyes will be sharper and you will be more aware of the way in which the artist was thinking when he made it. This is the real clue to appreciation.

Although I have been talking in terms of painting, you could, of course, study a piece of three-dimensional work, or visit a museum and look at ceramics and textiles.

In fact there is nothing new in this approach to studying art. No scientist would try to investigate a problem without reference to previous explorations in the same field and for hundreds of years artists have copied the works of their predecessors in order to examine and understand them better. A fascinating book called *Themes and Variations* has been published on this subject by Thames and

Above left
Pencil study of a detail from a Persian miniature painting. (12)

Above
Watercolour study made from the original oil painting by Renoir in the Courtauld Institute Galleries, London. Careful notes about colours were added to the analysis of the structure in a pencil drawing first. (14)

Left
A clay model based on Picasso's painting *The Three Musicians*. (16)

Opposite
Collage, chalks, string and cellophane were used to reconstruct this portrait by Picasso. (17)

Hudson. The illustrations show paintings and drawings which great artists have derived from the work of other artists. Amongst the examples is a drawing from a painting by Giotto which was made by Michelangelo when he was a boy of fourteen, drawings which Rembrandt made from Raphael, studies of Rembrandt's work by Van Gogh and Picasso's interpretations of El Greco and Velasquez.

If you can borrow this book from your library, you will see clearly how the character of the artist is reflected in the copy that he makes.

Make your own collection

You can make your own art collection by hunting for photographs, postcard reproductions and colour slides. Most galleries and museums publish reproductions of the works in their possession (some even allow you to use your own camera to take colour slides) and you can often see photographs in colour supplements and magazines.

Decide on how to arrange your collection. For reproductions and photographs you could use cardboard boxes, office box-files or plastic picnic boxes or you could stick everything into scrapbooks. The advantage of using boxes is that you can take things out separately to pin on a display board. You need to choose a method of sorting into groups and here are some possible ways of doing this:

a *Subjects:* portraits, landscape, still-life, etc.
b *Countries:* Italy, France, England, America, Japan etc.
c *Methods:* mosaic, drawing, sculpture, etc.
d *Periods:* Classical Greek, medieval, Victorian, etc.

There are, of course, some superb art books available: browse through the art section of a good bookshop and visit your local library to find books which especially interest you. Biographical studies of the life and work of one artist are usually easier to read; and books with large close-up details should be especially sought after. They really help you to see.

Collect books and reproductions to cover a broad period of time right up to the present day so that you can begin to see how all artists, of whatever period, are using a similar basic language while expressing different ideas that reflect their own surroundings and approach to life.

You will find it easier to understand this if you make your own drawings from works of art that you enjoy looking at. I have already suggested a method of studying a painting: this method could be applied to other forms of art; pottery, carving, sculpture, textiles, embroidery, costumes, furniture—in fact anything that particularly interests you. Drawing in galleries or museums brings you into direct contact with the originals but if this is not possible you can still learn a lot by drawing from reproductions.

Choose one that shows the details clearly. Work to any size and in any materials that seem appropriate for what you have chosen. The most important thing to remember is to observe just as carefully when drawing from a reproduction as you would if you were looking at an original. Making your own studies in this way will add a special, personal quality to your collection.

Everyday things

I suppose I am interested, above all, in investigating the golden ability of the artist to achieve a metamorphosis of quite ordinary things into something wonderful and extraordinary—the sublime of everyday life.

Roditi, 'Dialogues on Art'

Visual choices are not only the concern of painters and sculptors, they also concern the designers of all the man-made things which surround us. These are the things that we take so much for granted that it may not occur to us that someone had to make decisions about their size, shape, colour, material and purpose—in other words, design decisions.

We are more aware of this when we go into a shop to choose from a number of things on display. Suppose you are going to buy a chair: you sit in one to find out how comfortable it is and you touch it to get the feeling of the materials of which it is made. You will also want to stand back to appreciate its size, shape and colour.

In these ways you are testing your reactions to the decisions made by the designer. Your reactions to the abstract qualities of texture, shape and colour will depend on your own sensitivity to these qualities. This book suggests ways in which sensitivity can be developed through drawing and painting. Learning to assess your own work through your own experience will help you, in a similar way, to distinguish between well and badly-designed objects on sale in the shops.

What I have said about choosing a chair applies to all the other things which you have to choose from. We think about what they feel like and whether we like the shape and colour, and how they will relate to other objects. Clothes are an obvious example, as are all the furnishings in our homes.

At the moment you may not feel responsible for your surroundings but at some time you will be involved in making decisions about the design of your own home. You will have to select colour schemes, fabrics, furniture and floor coverings, and probably do your own painting and decorating and construct furniture and fitments.

You may like to look through catalogues and magazines for examples of designs that interest you. Cut them out and pin them up on a board in your room. This will help you to appreciate the differences in the designs and to discover why you feel that some are more pleasing than others. Whether you are collecting examples of cars, motor-bikes, clothes, radios or furniture, you can look for similar design problems in each of them. If you collect pictures of various cars, compare their shapes and the arrangement of details like the radiator, lamps and dashboard. Notice how different colours can affect the look of two cars of the same design. When you unpin the pictures, you could add them to your scrapbook.

Besides these things that we ourselves choose from, there are all the other designs which make up the structure of our cities. Occasionally beautiful old buildings are preserved, and new imaginative ones are built, but all too often our surroundings are spoiled through lack of sensitive planning and the pressures of commercial demand. Later in life you may find yourself in a position where you have to influence an important decision about the design and position of a new building. It would be your responsibility to think carefully and to make your decision in *visual terms*.

So far we have thought only about the design in everyday objects and buildings, but design affects us in other ways as well. When watching television you see images on the screen which have been designed by the director and cameraman working together. As in looking at a page of a book, it is easy to believe that what we see just 'happened' to arrive on the screen, or on the page, without any deliberate effort. In fact a television production requires an immense amount of planning as does the layout of a book. When you next watch television, try to be aware of the kind of problems that are involved— the positions of the cameras, the lighting of the set, and the particular emphasis to be given to each moment on the screen.

All this is overwhelmingly the concern of the film director. The story and characters may catch our interest at once, but the secret of a memorable film, as of a memorable painting, lies in the way the mind of the designer has worked to produce it. The same is true of photography. A snapshot of friends at the seaside is fun to have as a souvenir but a really good photograph needs the same organization of visual qualities as that which makes up a good painting. The designer recognizes these qualities and he knows how to use the camera to record them.

Design affects everything we see in the world around us. Even the countryside is affected by decisions: not only the decisions of town-planners and architects but also the way in which the farmer plants trees and hedges and grows his crops. We make similar decisions on a small scale when we plant flowers and shrubs and design the layout of our own gardens.

You can see that design is not confined within the walls of museums and galleries. It is part of our daily lives. An object as small as a teaspoon, or as large as a bridge, if it is well-designed, is a pleasure both to look at and to use. Design decisions demand an understanding of the visual qualities involved. I hope that this book will help you not only to enjoy drawing and painting, but also to appreciate these qualities as well.

Opposite

A collection of groceries inspired this painting of everyday things. Notice how each shape in the picture, including the arrangement of the lettering on the packets, contributes to the total structure of the design. (18)

This book is only a beginning and, although you have come to the end of it, you have not discovered all there is to understand about art. You have followed some lines of inquiry, and now it is up to you to investigate further.

You may wonder if you are making progress. Give yourself time. Development happens slowly, not in days, but over many months. Persevere and draw constantly and you will gradually see the visual world open up before your eyes.

Besides the marks of progress in your work there are the less tangible changes that occur within you. I hope you will agree that it is really no use trying to put ínto words the pleasure of learning to see, and that each creative experience stretches your mind and extends your awareness in all kinds of directions. Of course there will be times when you feel frustrated and defeated by a problem, but this is only to be expected. What will surprise you is your capacity to begin again. This is how we all make new discoveries and find our own individual routes to follow.

I hope that this book will encourage you to be yourself. Enjoy what you do. Beware of aiming for technical proficiency without feeling. Most of you can acquire techniques but this in itself is not enough. Far more important is the search for your own personal ideas and your own creative experience. Discover these things for yourself and you will have an endless source of satisfaction and enjoyment for the rest of your life.

Index

KING ALFRED'S COLLEGE
LIBRARY

Glossary of English and American terms

card:	poster board
cartridge paper:	drawing paper
cow gum:	rubber cement
drawing pin:	thumb tack
dressmaking pins:	straight pins
glass paper:	fine sand paper
guillotine:	paper cutter
gummed strips:	packing tape or masking tape
hessian:	canvas
lino:	linoleum
polycell:	cellulose based wallpaper paste
polythene sheet:	plastic drop cloth
P.V.A.	Elmer's glue
sellotape:	Scotch tape
squared maths paper:	graph paper
'Stanley' knife:	'mat' knife
sugar paper:	construction paper